Love, Your Beauty Godmother

By Blyss Macias

LOVE, YOUR BEAUTY GODMOTHER

To the women young or old not blessed with the community, the mothers, and the leaders I had; To anyone just looking for that extra guidance in their beauty journey.

May this voice be that direction, a safe space, and your biggest cheerleader!

Hello Gorgeous,

I'm so glad to be writing to you.

Like me, you may be tired of everyone having an opinion on how you should look, feel, and just exist. Every screen and underlying societal pressure pushes you towards impossible beauty standards with no direction on how to get there.

Society at large isn't focused on what is healthy. The simple act of opening your phone creates too many opportunities for insecurities to set in, for comparisons to arise, and for pressures to compromise who you are—all for you to just feel somewhat pretty, let alone beautiful. Issues plaguing the discovery of beauty are sadly a normal experience. Those experiences may have tainted your relationship with beauty (or even impacting how you see yourself). My hope is that this tainted relationship and the glorification of an unrealistic ideal ends when you read this book.

The beauty world can be a wild one. There are so many options and opportunities for creativity and expression, every turn a new colorful path. I have spent years in the salon, working as a stylist, business owner, and makeup artist. I've had a hand in everything from fashion shows, to elaborate theater productions, to the most intimate weddings. This experience, combined with all of the "salon therapy" that goes on when a client is in the chair, has let me in on all kinds of industry secrets. I am writing to you to *share* a secret with you.

Take these stories and secrets to heart. Learn from my experiences, successes, and mistakes. If you'll take the time to be introspective, experiment with new beliefs, and maybe even be a little daring by implementing new tools, then the word "beauty" will mean something very different to you than it may right now. I believe you will cherish that word, be empowered by it, and even identify with it.

Cheers to your beauty journey.

Love,

Your Beauty Godmother

Table of Contents

Introduction

Beauty has always been near and dear to my heart even as I was working out my own journey of how beauty belonged in me. As I have been on that beauty journey, I found I could not keep all the amazing benefits and confidence true beauty brought me to myself. I needed to share it. I needed to shift the standard.

One of the most significant moments in this journey was when I realized I *had* to open my own business.

I remember the day when the name for it came to me.

A typical, busy day working at a high end salon began with a quiet morning. I'd buy a muffin and a latte from the coffee shop next door and open the shop with about three other stylists. I'd prepare some hot towels, get my tickets with the list of clients for the day, and set up my station. More stylists would begin trickling in, and by the afternoon, the salon was buzzing.

Salons have a particular hum to them, dynamic conversations happening from chair to chair as clients are connecting with their stylists. Water from the shampoo bowls flowing, blow dryers running, the rhythm of sweeping, all collide for the symphony that is the salon atmosphere. I love it. Honestly, even the break room is usually not that quiet, but is still a safe haven when you're having lunch.

I remember sitting in that break room one afternoon, probably eating a chicken, caesar salad from a local shop I was obsessed with. I had been contemplating throughout the day. Some of my close friends, and many of my clients, recently mentioned I should open my own salon. This topic was becoming a recurring conversation, and it seemed like everyone was in agreement. Everyone except me.

I never had the desire to open my own salon; it sounded like an unnecessary responsibility added to my already overloaded schedule. I didn't feel I fit the mold of the beauty world. I loved fashion, creativity, and expression in make-up, style, and hair. The more over-the-top, the better. However, when I looked around at other stylists, beauty professionals/influencers, celebrity artists—I just didn't fit in. I didn't have the same priorities.

Doing hair has never been just a job to me. Unlike many of my colleagues, I didn't get into hair as a stepping stone or side gig while I finished my degree. Even my conversations with stylists about dating and life outside the salon didn't always click. For the most part, the culture of the beauty industry is pretty people making money and causing drama. Living like rockstars—sex, drugs, and partying on the weekends—then living off of caffeine and one meal a day during the week. Too often people, especially those in the beauty industry, buy into the lie that being "good looking" and living in a way that "looks good" and exciting is all there is to life.

I loved being in the salon. There was always something else to discover, but I never found my one thing. I earned the title of "master colorist." Eventually, my obsession with learning brought me to a "cutting specialist," but I could never really narrow down one thing in the craft. I just loved the art of beauty.

And I loved my clients.

Even if their service was a super simple one color touch-up, I was excited to see the women in my chair. I loved hearing their stories, asking how they met their spouse, talking about their favorite restaurant—simple things.

On this particular day, a new client came to see me. Well, she was new to me, but not to the salon. The other stylists scowled as soon as they heard her name. They were quick to tell stories from previous experiences, and opinions on what I should look out for. Talk about second-hand anxiety. I started getting nervous, playing out terrible scenarios in my head for this client I hadn't even met!

However, as soon as she sat down, I could tell my fellow stylists were just being gossipy. This woman had nothing but love for people, but she had a very hard time valuing herself. She raved about her kids for the entire appointment, her eyes beaming with how proud she was of them. Her marriage was in a tough spot. There was a lot of disconnection in the relationship. She wasn't angry, as many women would have been; she just wanted her and her husband to be close. She wanted him to be happy, to be fulfilled, and it broke her heart to not see him at his best. Her love for him, even when she was so disappointed, amazed me. Everyone she talked about she adored.

But the conversation would shift anytime I would ask her about herself.

There are many things that could be causing her self hate—trauma from her childhood, or just being beaten down by life. She was so negative, she was making herself sick. In the short time we spent together, I discovered she'd been bombarded by illness, both mental and physical, for years. Hearing it all, no wonder people thought she was a little uptight at times. The poor thing hadn't had a normal life in years! She felt helpless, misunderstood, and lost. As a Christian, all I wanted to do was hug her, pray over her, and tell her how amazing she was. I thought through every resource I had access to. Were there any doctors I knew? Could I get a pastor to pray with her? Was there a book on self image or self love 101? Could I pull from inventory and give her a free drink? My thoughts were reeling. How could I show this woman some love and some hope? But I stopped short.

I had just recently gotten a talking-to from my boss about making people uncomfortable with my religious beliefs and not letting them seep into work. I was, "too positive and needed to let women rant or gossip in the chair if that's what they wanted to do." Who knew having positivity could be a bad thing? It really frustrated me. This woman could have used my help. She could have had a revolutionary solution, a new connection, or at the very least a different, positive view of herself. But all of that was somehow against work protocol? This made no sense to me. Weren't we, as stylists, the experts on true beauty? Wasn't it our job to make our clients feel better leaving the salon than they did when they first came in? I was going crazy trying to figure out how to do my job without losing my own identity and everything I believed in at the same time. As I thought about this encounter while I was in the break room, it hit me.

I *did* need to open my own business, and I needed to call that business "The Industry." Not because I was going to have the most prestigious salon, the highest quality customer service, or the best cutting edge techniques known to hairstylists far and wide (though those are goals of mine). My business would be called "The Industry" because it's bringing us back to the heart of what the beauty industry is supposed to be all about.

The beauty industry has monetized part of the human identity. Not that beauty professionals don't deserve to be paid, they are masters of image creativity—constantly learning, growing, and perfecting service and technique, all while adhering to the strictest health and safety law. Trendsetters, brand owners, marketing agencies, educators, celebrity platform artists, and eager assistants have all turned the business of helping people feel and look more beautiful into a global, multi-billion dollar industry. Why is it then that so many women still struggle with self-image and low self-esteem? How is it that so many of us have lost what true beauty within the identity of humanity really is?

The most important thing to me, even above the service I was doing or what I did in the breakroom, was the heart of my client that day. I wanted her to know the wonder of beauty was in her because of how she cared for people, and that when given the right space, her beauty would seep into everything else. The magic was already inside of her.

Just as the magic is in you. It always has been.

The fascination with beauty is not in the current advanced highlighting technique no one can agree on how to pronounce (you would be shocked at how many different ways people come up with to say the word balayage— baileyege, booleyage, bilogeyege—the list is honestly endless). The obsession is not in the new lipstick color, or even in the latest never-aging-fountain-of-youth procedure. *The magic is that you are wearing it.* Is anything really beautiful unless love and life are carrying it, unless you begin to embody it? There is nothing really groundbreaking going on in the foils.

I am shifting the focus.

Spinning the chair so you can really see what's important.

Pretty soon you will love what's staring back at you in the mirror.

Love,
Your Beauty Godmother

Chapter 1
What We See

I have this insatiable desire to change the way things are done. This desire bleeds into many areas of my life, but especially in regards to the beauty industry. My fascination with beauty started from a young age. I grew up around art, fashion, and makeup. I was raised by and around creative artists. Beauty was just art you could wear—an art that was you, an art that was endless.

I loved that princesses in the movies depicted their royalty and their culture in what they wore. Musicians had the wild make up and set design to immerse you in their songs. The women I knew always dressed up to celebrate events. I loved watching them find the colors that made their eyes pop, the shades that made their skin glow, and those crazy pants that made them feel like a million dollars.

I'm sure you have those favorite things as well. Maybe it's your most treasured accessory. It might be a simple lip color that makes you feel like you can take over the world. Fashion and cosmetics color the people walking down the street, making society more than a gray slate to look at. They draw us to certain spaces, allowing us to be a part of different atmospheres, and can even drive buying decisions. More than that, our style choices do something for us. When you decide to dress up to go to a nice event, there can be a lot of preparation involved. Planning the outfit, spending a little extra time on your hair or makeup, and any mental readiness needed to switch to a social environment. When you as a woman decide to go out and show up, prepared and excited, you are no longer in the event, at the restaurant, witnessing the celebration. You are a part of the event. You are adding presence in a primed and aligned way. In doing so, you endorse the event, making it that much more impactful.

The current beauty industry is not what beauty was originally meant to be. When you think of the beauty world, it's a breeding ground for comparison and insecurity. Perfect hair, lasered skin, fake body parts—all of these things are curated in a way to make you feel like you are not enough. In my interactions with the beauty world—the ads, the social media profiles—I often feel like I'm interacting with the matrix version of real people.

Everyone is trying to be the next "It" girl. Ironically, by attempting to be original, they all end up becoming the same person—picture perfect zombies.

Within the business of beauty, any good marketing professional will tell you that when you're making an ad, you present a problem and then solve it for the buyer. But what if they present the problem as *you*?

Don't you find it odd that most beauty ads present completely normal things like curves, acne, stretchmarks, body hair, or aging as a flaw? Most of us are aware that the photoshop techniques advertisers use are completely unrealistic. We *know* that mentally. We are also aware that the widespread usage of filters, editing, and photoshop, make the lack of these completely normal things the beauty norm. Even those with the strongest willpower can be subjected to comparing thoughts.

Many studies have shown that women, especially adolescent girls, feel worse about themselves and their appearance after seeing beauty advertisements, so much so that they want to *change* the way they look. This is the case even if they know the image is airbrushed or photoshopped. In a research report, "The Real Truth About Beauty: A Global Report," conducted by Dove in 2004, showed that on average, women see about 2000 advertisements a week, and most of those women don't see their beauty (people who look like them) reflected or represented in those ads. This study also revealed that "only 2% of women from around the world consider themselves beautiful." (https://www.clubofamsterdam.com/contentarticles/52%2 0Beauty/dove_white_paper_final.pdf)

The language in beauty advertisements is not, "What do you like about yourself and how can we enhance that?" Instead it is, "What flaw do you have and how can we help you hide it?" On average, you're seeing close to 300 ads a day that don't actually make you feel good about yourself. All those ads pose the questions: How do I be the one everyone wants? How do I buy this image?

It's ridiculous how even a tube of mascara is selling you on how to be the next sex idol. Every celebrity, music video, and social media influencer is implying there is something wrong with you. They're selling an insecure voice that tells you if you're not posed the right way, wearing the right thing, with the right haircut, and the right brand of makeup, then maybe you won't be accepted. Or loved. We've bought insecurity, and so we fear that if we leave the house without makeup on, society might think something is wrong with us.

How do you combat something as large as this version of the beauty industry? The current industry doesn't speak to who women are. It is over sexualized, image based, and unattainable. It's not natural or innate. It's a show. How do you go up against something like that? This always-present thought of not being enough, it is something I wanted to dismantle for *years*. It felt like an impossible mission.

Until one day, the solution came to me...

To combat and take down this monolith, the key is getting people to actually believe in themselves again.

Gorgeous woman, when you begin to believe in who you are, you allow yourself to be just that—yourself. You become real. You can't fabricate the genuine essence of someone. It's not something you can buy; it's something you become. What stands out in a crowd of perfect robots? A person who is real. A person who embodies a beauty that wakes you up to the truth that being alive is better than playing a role. To become this, you need to begin believing that you already are the thing you want to be, and then spend the rest of your life taking care of and building *that* person.

Every product you then encounter becomes a helpful tool to use or not to use. It is no longer an identity. I'm not saying we need to destroy the beauty industry as a whole. I just want to put the power back in your hands. I want to help you fall in love with the person you already are. If you do interact with the beauty industry, I want it to be something that serves you.

You already are beautiful. There is gold in you. Beauty is innate. Beauty is not about changing who you are; it's about enhancing and making who you are into someone who is functioning and healthy. When you get this part of beauty working properly, then attraction, relationships, and your life all come into alignment because it's part of who you are.

Beauty is healing. When you're around real true beauty, it can help you to relax. You feel safe. Furthermore, when you allow yourself to own your inner beauty, you become a safe person for those around you. You start to look for and pull out beautiful things that may have been buried if you were in an insecure state.

Beauty is something you deserve to embody and express. You are legitimately missing a part of yourself until you claim your beauty and fulfill your idea of self. Claiming your beauty allows you to take responsibility and celebrate yourself. You begin to move toward confidence. Until a woman feels confident in who she is, she'll be asking everyone else for that validation and sense of self worth. When you aren't confident in yourself, you make decisions that are not in line with who you really are. You make decisions to fit in, not based on what you want to do.

We're going to do something fun.

Relax for thirty seconds, and take a moment to imagine something with me. Picture yourself living your best life. Whatever that means to you. It could be going out on the town this weekend with your best friends. Traveling to a place you've always wanted to go. Walking into your dream home.

Go further, into the things that you want to accomplish. How do you see yourself hitting certain milestones? Picture yourself getting married. What does your life with that spouse look like? Maybe you want to be a parent. What cool things will you teach your kids to do? See those relationships. Focus on you living it out. What are *you* doing?

Let your mind wander.

Is there something you've always wanted to do? Remember, this is your best life. Go all out. Are you running a company? Are you leading people? Speaking on a grand stage? Being interviewed by prestigious people? Are you flying a plane? Driving your dream car? Are you pushing the limits on what your strength and athletic abilities can do? Accepting an award? Breaking records?

I don't want you to just picture one thing, or a couple scenarios. Picture life at its fullest. Visualize you living it. How does it feel? What are some of the emotions involved? Allow yourself to experience it.

Can you see it?

What you just imagined is who you are. That is your most beautiful life.

Does that person you just watched live your best life, match the person you see in the mirror? Why or why not? What can we do to get you closer to those two pictures becoming one? Our goal is to get that vision and your reality into alignment, so they become the same picture.

Identity is not a game where you get a character card listing traits from your genetics, culture, and online personality test results. It's more like a deep well within you. As you age, you continue to delve deeper into the well and discover more of who you really are.

What you imagined in that envisioning exercise is you. The potential for that dream life *is already in you.* As you dig and grow, you unearth deeper realities of that identity.

I use this envisioning exercise often to help me be at peace with who I am. It helps me to strengthen the path I am on because I'm asking myself questions like: Can I be really confident in what I am doing? Do I need to adjust a little bit to get back to my authentic self?

Doing this exercise can also help me recognize and celebrate when my vision matches my reality. I remember a distinct moment when this happened for me. It was one of the first times I was paid to speak at a three day conference for youth.

Speaking is something I enjoy doing. I love engaging with people. I love planning the outfits. Communicating effectively to a large group of people is a crazy experience. There's a rush of adrenaline right before you walk up—a nervousness that you might say the wrong thing, or not look the way you want to. Once you smile and start speaking, however, the audience is no longer just the audience. You are all in it together. It is incredible feeling so connected to so many people in one moment.

There was a moment in the middle of the conference I loved. Someone in the audience had filmed a clip of me on stage and tagged me in it on social media. It was maybe thirty seconds long. I remember watching it. At first, it felt weird. Sometimes seeing yourself on camera can be a funny experience, especially when it's not what you expected. Most of the time when I've seen clips of myself speaking, I'll notice the material on my jacket doesn't look the way I thought it would under the stage lights, or I won't be aware that my voice sounded as serious as it actually did.

This thirty second clip struck me because I didn't have any of those thoughts. I watched the video and said, "That's exactly how I saw myself doing that!" There was not a difference between the picture I had in my mind, envisioning myself on stage speaking, and the actual footage of me living it out.

That felt so good, and took a lot of pressure off of me going into the next session. I felt like I was doing what I was supposed to be doing at the moment, in the way I was supposed to do it.

The concept of acting in alignment and being consistent with who you are in every area of your life is taught a lot by business professionals. When you make decisions that are in line with the core of who you are, things flow much more easily. There is also an added sense of joy because you're making decisions you want to follow through with, as opposed to making decisions based on pressure, fear, or convenience. When you are acting in alignment, there is no disconnect or inconsistency in your being. Being in alignment is being the woman you envisioned, your most fulfilled and most beautiful self. The version of you that you see when you imagine your future, that's the woman you can become! Moreover, the sooner you get to fully embodying her, the closer you will be to living the life you want, having the relationships you want to have, and feeling at home in your body.

It's the concept of self-actualization—realizing all your potential, recognizing your talents and strengths, and then leaning into everything you are capable of. You need to see yourself as successful and fulfilled. The view you have of yourself is the reality you are pulling yourself into. Do not paint a picture of your greatest fears and worries. You will drag yourself into a negative existence. You need to see yourself as beautiful. Let that vision of your best self come to the surface. Allow yourself to dream about it and experience it. Then begin to walk into it.

Questions from Your Beauty Godmother

1. *How do you envision your best life? Write it out and title it "Most beautiful life" if you like. Be as detailed as you can:*

Dedicate some time to really dream and develop the vision you saw of yourself. Dream about what is possible. Keep a running document or journal you can come back to and remind yourself of that vision and goal. Add to it as more dreams come up. The more detailed you are in writing this down, and the more you revisit it, the more natural the process will be as you become that dream woman within you.

2. *What do you like about yourself?*

Keep adding to this list and compliment yourself in the mirror. Do this as often as possible. Make it a morning routine if you have to. The goal is for you to become aware of your beauty and to be intentional with loving and nurturing yourself as you grow into the woman you envisioned.

Chapter 2
Peeling Off The Mask

Masking is comparing and hiding the genuine you. It's taking what you see in other people, and wearing it as your own. I'm not talking about relationship building or empathy. I'm talking about, "Well that hairstyle worked for her, so now I want the exact same one." Or, "Men seem to like her lips or her nose, so I'll get surgery to look like that." When you notice comments or thoughts like that starting to pop up, with no regard for how those things actually fit who you are, ask yourself, "How will this affect *my* beauty?" Will it really enhance you and bring you closer to the ideal version of yourself that *you* envisioned, or does it hide you? Masking is a copy, paste attitude. It creates a facade of an identity that doesn't truly belong to you.

My mother is a gorgeous woman. She's exotic, crafty, artistic, and has always had this gift of making anything and everything aesthetically special with just the materials she has on hand.

We could be outright broke, living in the worst part of town, in the smallest lot available, eating top ramen for weeks, and all the other moms would be envious of where we lived, stealing ideas on how to make their Christmas tree look as good as ours. One of the awesome things about apartment communities is all the kids hang out together, and a parent is typically an earshot away. Somehow, we all end up in each other's living rooms at one point or another.

One year, all of us neighborhood kids were running around from one end of the complex to the other, stopping in at my apartment to get water or snacks. The kids were so stunned that the inside of our unit looked so nice and felt so welcoming. They didn't want to go back outside. A few of the kids even brought their moms back later to look at our kitchen set up and Christmas decor, and to ask my mom for tips on how to make their home look similar.

My mom was never really into designer brands, but she always presented very well. Etiquette school, modeling, and acting from her youth all translated into how she carried herself. She thought if she appeared well, all would be well, and for the most part, that worked.

Unfortunately the things she valued—presentation, beauty, and giftings—began to turn into an ingenuine performance of insecurity and fear. I adopted this pattern of behavior and eventually had to break it in myself as well.

Facades don't fill emptiness. I remember watching my mom, this beautiful, seemingly all together woman, practically beg for compliments and feed on the attention and flirtation of any man, even though she was a married woman. Looks can't fix everything. I wish I knew that growing up. I wish I knew my beauty wasn't limited to what others see in me.

As young women discovering the world, we begin to map out who we are by the impact situations had on us, where we live, and what those around us had to say.

If there is a presence of undealt with rejection causing self doubt, or fear, everything else is just used as something to mask it—even things like talent, validation, or approval of others. I saw this in my own life. Qualities I had, that were actually strengths, were turned into weaknesses if I was moving in insecurity.

For example, creativity is a strength of mine. Both of my parents are creative. A lot of my artistry comes from my mom. One of the giftings she helped me develop is being able to replicate almost anything I see, whether that's on a canvas or for a particular cosmetic look. I loved fashion and makeup as a young girl, and I learned a lot of skills from friends and YouTube. I can make myself look like nearly anyone. Growing up, part of this strength (the artistic creative side) was personality, and part of it (the camouflage for acceptance) was presentation.

We moved around a lot growing up. I always made friends quickly, but I began to feel like I never belonged anywhere. Insecurity grew as I started to see that what was so important in some communities, didn't really matter to others. What one city said was cool, another city laughed at. It became impossible to fit everyone's standards. I started to live in fear of not getting it right.

At some point, I realized I was performing and that I had to stop. I eventually made the decision that fitting in didn't matter. Instead of blending in like a chameleon, I just took what I liked from each group and made my own person. This gave me a lot of freedom and a lot of confidence. It helped me understand and see many different types of people. I had to let relationships steep long enough for me to see if they really valued me or if they just liked the role I played and the image I brought to their life. I had to be okay with not being everyone's favorite.

Correcting different patterns is a journey that sometimes is dealt with in layers. Later, when I got into ministry and started leading younger women, I began to see how deep some of the performance masking really ran. Even wearing the mask of "being a good person," and "never doing anything wrong" didn't let people see the real me (which ultimately damaged them). I had to deal with deeper layers of insecurity.

Masking can be anything you hide behind to cover your genuine and authentic self. Removing the mask can look superficial, like when I realized having a different fashion expression actually freed me to be who I am, or it can be deeper, like when I allowed myself to lead through vulnerability. It's all layers of the same thing. You do not have to bare your deepest darkest secrets to everyone, but if you notice something is being used as a mask and hindering your ability to engage your most authentic self, take a moment to pause. Remember the woman you are wanting to become and respond from that place.

The real freedom, the trueness of beauty, happens when you know who you are. Explore your strengths and talents. What do you love about yourself? What activities really light you up? What are you passionate about? What do others compliment you on? Then match the image on the outside to your heart on the inside. That's when you really come alive. Until then, all of this beauty work is just a pretty veneer.

I'm not going to teach you how to just suck it up, put on a pretty face, and carry on. That's a necessary skill for the competitive workplace and needed in certain seasons, but not when it comes to beauty.

Beauty is tough. It is absolutely strong, but it is not brute force (and it certainly is not fake). It comes from the hard work of knowing yourself. It comes from cultivating real strength in being vulnerable and allowing your true self to emerge. Beauty runs deeper than the compliments of others.

Everyone wants to be the "it" girl, but she doesn't really exist. She's a character in a scripted role of a made up story.

Think about it. You don't really want to be the star in every job position. You don't want to take everyone's boyfriend. You want the things, the job positions, and the people that are meant *for you*—the things that fall into alignment with your true, beautiful self.

It's so damaging to your confidence, decision making, and even the way you view the world, if you accept this "it" girl mentality.

It is fun to be the center of attention every once in a while—to wear the knock out dress, all eyes on you. There are very valid times to be acknowledged and celebrated, but it's a very dangerous thing to believe the lie that if you are not the "it" girl, you are not important.

I have a long time friend who is incredibly talented, beautiful, and sweet. She always struggled with confidence, but I didn't realize how much until she met her now husband.

They're happily married and doing great, but when they first met, she couldn't see how much he really liked her. She continuously discounted her own beauty and discredited his pursuit of her, which was so obvious to the rest of us. She would say things like, "He only talks to me to get to someone else in the group," and "I'm not the pretty girl everyone wants." At the end of the day, it didn't matter that she wasn't this imaginary "it" girl everyone wanted. She was the one *he* wanted. She was his "it" girl. Every time he talked to the rest of us, it was to obsess over how much he liked her.

Don't try to be the girl everyone wants (that's impossible). Be the one you choose.

Beauty isn't really taught, so it's easy to default to messages the media bombards us with. Most people are getting their idea of beauty from distorted resources. One of the biggest perpetrators is the internet with the way it showcases companies trying to sell you on a product or an image. At its core, this distortion is an attack on identity and what it means to be a woman. Before social media was selling you a product, culture was selling us an idea. Hollywood has never failed to tell us who the next sex symbol is and how we can aim to look like her. Disney told us that the pretty princess would always be the one to find love.

It's not the truth. It's an ideal created by something else that doesn't necessarily reflect who you are.

It's normal for you to hit moments (or even seasons) where you don't feel the best (that's just life), but part of this process of discovering your beauty is taking ownership of who you are rather than letting circumstances, moments, or people tell you who you are. Be true to *your* identity. Think about what your definition of beauty is. Is it a standard you carry yourself in? Is it a recurring image you see in women or the world around you? What influenced this idea of beauty? Was it your family? Your culture? A particular event or movie that resonated with you? Then think about your answers to the previous questions with the vision of your "Most Beautiful Life." Are there any conflicting mindsets or limiting beliefs you need to let go of? Identify anything holding you back or contradicting your ultimate vision. Letting go of, healing from, and replacing these mindsets will help you be more congruent within yourself and get you closer to your most beautiful life.

If you need to own a mistake, take ownership of it, but don't stay in it. Figure out the distractions. Figure out what things or ideals you're chasing that are not in alignment with what you're supposed to do.

Also, pay attention to when you do feel beautiful.

In the article, "Neural Plasticity: 4 Steps to Change Your Brain & Habits," Dr.Kim states,
"Mental activity strengthens the neural pathways in your brain associated with what you focus on with your thoughts and feelings...—if you focus on happiness [or beauty] with your thoughts and feelings, you strengthen [beauty] pathways."

Scientifically, when you think on something over and over, you create stronger mental pathways around that subject. The more you do this, the easier it is for your brain to associate with that subject and create a belief that affects your feelings and actions.

Have you ever gotten a really good hairstyle or cut and said, "I feel like me." That's how you know a particular hairstyle is aligned with your identity. That's why we each part our hair a certain way. That's why we each gravitate towards different styles of clothes. Yes, you can refine or adjust based on the professional setting or different season, but start with you. Ask more questions. Do you really want to be blonde, or do you just want to feel brighter? Do you really want to look like her, or do you just want to be softer? Do you really want those friends, or do you just want the connections they have? Do you really like him, or do you just want male attention? There's no wrong answer, but you do need to know.

There will always be room for improvement. When you have a goal to reach, a place you have not been before, or something new you want to try, it will always be a little uncomfortable at first. You will not be an expert at it right away. Still, when you're at least going in the direction of the vision you have of yourself, there is a magnetic pull attached to it. When things within you are in congruence with each other (even if they're not perfect or the "final product"), they begin to flow together. You become massively confident and relaxed in your decisions. You might be working at something, but you're not striving.

You need to start with you.

This will keep you from making one dimensional, emotion-based decisions. It also allows the real you to come alive.

Questions from your Beauty Godmother

1. *Thinking about masks as insecurities we hide behind, are there any masks you are currently using instead of engaging the most authentic you?*

Remember that masks can be superficial like something you literally wear, or more deep and internal like a belief system, you may also have different masks for different situations.

2. *When was a time where you felt truly beautiful?*

Again, be as detailed as possible. Look for ways to incorporate contributing factors into your day to day routine to recreate opportunities for you to walk in this as much as possible.

Chapter 3
The Danger of not Embodying Your Beauty

Unfortunately, my childhood was a dark one. I spent so long ripping myself away from self-deprecating insecurity, counterfeit powers, and false validation. I spent so much time getting back my stolen identity and working through the fear of becoming my true self, but I'm not afraid of that anymore. I'm not afraid of myself. Darkness tried to take and corrupt my innate beauty (just as it's trying to do with yours), so have no problem helping you take your beauty back from the darkness too.

There is a story about the infamous angel Lucifer. His name literally means "the star of the morning." He's described as the seal of perfection, full of wisdom, and perfect in beauty, wearing every precious stone. Commissioned to guard and protect the throne of God, this angel was meant to be an inspiration, a shining light pointing to how awesome and wonderful God is. However, Lucifer let his high rank and beauty cause pride in him, which eventually turned to jealousy and selfishness. Instead of using his giftings and beauty to bring harmony, safety, and joy to God and others, he went after the boss's job. His pride became so great, it corrupted him, twisted the glory in him, and made him evil. Because of this, he and his followers (who were also driven by corrupt motives) were thrown out of heaven. (Ezekiel 28, Isaiah 14, Revelation 12)

There's an allure to the darkness. It has its own kind of beauty. There's a craving for the forbidden. Lucifer was beautiful. He was the bright morning star, emanating perfection. That type of beauty shifts atmospheres. It invokes feeling. It's not just pleasing to look at, it's radiating energy. Still just like the story of Lucifer, when you take that beauty, and make it self centered it turns dark. Instead of healthy life giving beauty, surrendered to something greater, a dark and corrupted beauty will claw at glory or light. It will ruin, defile and tear down anything that does not adore itself. It's unnatural, painful even, yet you can't look away. It's a trap. You know it's a trap. It looks, sounds, and even feels like a trap. You almost want to be trapped by it.

True beauty is life giving, peaceful, and radiant. It is nurturing, refreshing, and healing. In its purest form, beauty connects us to heaven and eternity. When it's corrupted, beauty clings the seduction of darkness. Today we have beauty without God or heaven—no rules, no guides, no light, and certainly no care for others. If we are not taught true and eternal beauty, we are left to our own devices and broken resources, trying to conjure anything to get us close to the smoke of the true fire. We're left to just make it up as we go. That's what brands, businesses, influencers, and stylists are doing—just making it up.

As I mentioned before, my childhood was dark. It wasn't all bad. For the most part, I grew up with two parents in the same household who did the very best they could raising myself and my sisters with the resources they had. Even from a young age, I had a lot of intuition, and a sensitivity to people and their energies. I really, really cared about people.

I was also misled. Untrustworthy voices hijacked a lot of the giftings and strengths I had. I got lost in witchcraft, giving into dark influences, and conjured demons.

That lifestyle robbed me of a lot, exposing me to a great deal of trauma early on. I felt like my significance was only wrapped up in what I did, which tied a lot of my identity to performing for other people. Because my focus was so lasered in on doing, and not on healing or processing well with safe voices, all my interactions with (and the impact I had on) people became incredibly negative. I dealt with feeling misunderstood and insecure, acting out violently, and having to manufacture false confidence. I was really just trying to survive during most of that time. My belief in myself got buried away.

Since that time, I've healed a lot and have been able to give those misused giftings and strengths a new redeemed meaning. Part of the journey of picking up the pieces of my identity was refining beauty, how it pertains to me, and what I use it for.

After I removed myself from that lifestyle, I still carried a lot of shame around beauty. I had a hard time seeing beauty as a *good* thing because, in the past, I always used it as a tool to gain something from people, or I associated it with people who were abusive. Some of that ideology was learned from patterns in my mom's insecurities, but also the darkness I was involved with turned beauty into a seductive commodity—something that was only recognized when needed for leverage.

It *felt* like a negative thing to be attractive. It wasn't until I pinpointed where those beliefs came from, released the situation that created the belief, and forgave (myself and others) that I was finally able to start enjoying beauty again.

Your story may not be as intense or as dark as mine (or it might be). Ultimately that doesn't matter. We all have grown up with negative messages about beauty and how it should be used. The world of beauty can feel a lot like walking into a scene from *Alice in Wonderland*. It's wild, colorful, and thrilling, but it can also be very confusing, and heartbreaking if you don't know who you are. Identifying the negative beliefs you have around beauty in your own mind will help you to heal and embody beauty the way you should.

When people tell me, "Oh, I could never rock that hairstyle," or "I could never pull off that hair color," most of the time they aren't even thinking about that actual hairstyle. Sometimes it is a concern on whether or not it will fit their face shape or compliment their skin tone. More often than not, when I ask more questions, they're thinking about the lifestyle they associate with the hairstyle. What is the first thing that comes to mind when you think about the word platinum? Is it money? Do you associate that with a particular status? What about the first thing that comes to mind when you see a shiny haired model? Most people think of high fashion, or the Grammys. Whatever the reason, when people begin to discredit themselves, it is rooted in some type of identity issue.

Somewhere along the way, beauty turned into a lifeless idol. Something told us beauty was something we didn't have and that we needed to work very hard to get it. The standard has always been miles away. The beauty industry started creating fake people—personas constantly performing and dressing up, rather than being comfortable in their own skin. This causes a fracture in people's identity at best, and at worst, it creates complete alter egos of people. That's why so many people have so many weird alter egos everywhere they go. Work life versus personal life. A social media account for the public, and a private account for close friends. Now, there are some roles you have to step into in the professional world, or a needed style of communication you should be utilizing for certain situations (you don't speak to a toddler the same way you would a thirty-year-old adult), but there is a core of who you are that needs to be integrous.

Not embodying your beauty is dangerous. When you are not honest with yourself, and carry too many personas, it puts an exhausting demand on your life that you were never meant to carry. It affects what you do to get ready in the morning, how you interact with other people, and sets limits on your life because you're trying to fit into someone else's box. Somewhere along the way, you began to believe beauty was outside of you, that it was a foreign language you needed to learn. Something told you that you were just one degree off, that there was just one more thing to change, one more thing to give up. If you hide just one more flaw, you'll have it. You'll be just like them. You'll be beautiful.

It's all a lie.

Begin to search your own feelings, reactions, and story to find the things that may be keeping you from knowing your true self and stepping into your beauty. You shouldn't have to pretend. This is a journey of honesty, learning, and growing that woman you see in your mind. Embodying beauty takes time. It doesn't have a shortcut.

It's also not something you can buy. The lie has been that beauty is not something you have, but rather it's someone you need to become or something you need to spend money on to get. The truth is you *do* have beauty.

Things in the material world function the opposite of how people think they do. Whether it's wealth, relationships, or beauty, the principles behind these are the same. People don't begin life with the flashy car. They don't get married because of the honeymoon. Fitness models don't start with a sculpted body. These results happened because people actively worked towards them. Good hair takes time. Good products are an investment, and a healthy body takes discipline, but I'm talking about something deeper. When you were born, you were already made with beauty inside you. It's part of your DNA. You were designed with glory, goodness, and uniqueness.

Beauty absolutely should be admired, desired, and something we put great care into. In fact, you *need* to put care into it. When you deny your beauty, you cut off and deny a part of yourself. It's inherent in women. It is in everything we do. It's in the *way* we do things. The fact that every little detail from your nail color, the way you arrange your home, to the way you speak can be beautiful is something of great wonder. You are it already, and you are allowed to cultivate it into your life.

I want you to discover, enjoy, and build who you are—making that person ever more healthy. You should do more of what refreshes you. Take more time for soul care. You don't have to buy into what is trendy. You don't have to like what everyone else likes. Being authentically you is where this all starts, where beauty begins, where confidence will grow from, and where living the way you want to will meet you. It starts with simple things. For instance, I don't drink caffeine. I'm not gonna write this book in a hipster coffee shop. It's not who I am. I'm going to go to the bougiest restaurant I can go to, get a cocktail, jam out to some energetic music, and get it done.

If you don't decide to be your genuine authentic self, you spend your whole life unhappy. You will not spend it living on purpose. You will not spend it with the people who are actually for you. You spend your whole life playing a role.

It's exhausting.

It's dangerous.

When you are not acting intentionally, you are not living in your purpose as a woman. How are you going to live out your most beautiful life if you don't even know who you are? Knowing who you are affects how you're going to fulfill that vision and impact the people you care about. I don't think believing or not believing in your beauty will directly impact your overall purpose and grand scale impact on the world, but I do think it will greatly affect how you go about it and how you feel about yourself while living that purpose out. Women feeling beautiful isn't the answer to everything, but it is the answer to a lot. At the very least, it brings you to an inner peace where you can find the answers you need to do whatever it is you're on this earth to do.

Questions from your Beauty Godmother

1. *What are some of your favorite things? When is the last time you allowed yourself to enjoy these things?*

List out the things that bring you joy (i.e. your favorite dessert, your favorite kind of music, your favorite places to go etc.)

2. *What are some characteristics you are really strong in?*

You can list things you are really good at and things you really enjoy doing. You can also list your top strengths, and moments you really see those strengths being played out. If you haven't taken the Gallup Strengthsfinder test, I highly suggest you do. It can be an awesome tool to discover a lot of great things about yourself.

3. *What do you feel purposed to do? Or currently feel purpose in?*

A good way to discover this is by asking yourself what you feel passionate about. What do you feel frustration around, so much so that you want to do something to bring a solution to it? What causes you to grow the most? What do you find fulfillment in? Asking yourself these questions, and involving yourself more and more in those answers, will help you to be more on purpose in your everyday life.

Chapter 4
Untangling Real Beauty

If I could personify beauty, she would be a very powerful, yet very gracious, gentle woman, confident in her body and the world around her. When interacting with her, I feel closer to God and more secure in myself. She is physically attractive, very striking, but somehow becomes more beautiful as I get to know her. To know all her emotions, as she expresses them in a healthy way, brings freedom to my own heart. When she talks about God and spiritual things, which are usually complicated and vague, it sounds simple. What used to feel otherworldly, now feels like home. She is somehow ancient, like she exists outside of time. Yet every culture and era would praise her, beyond trend or preference. She doesn't wear armor, yet she cannot be harmed. This is beauty, who sits in vibrant color and lends her wisdom, who by simply walking, defeats the fiercest of enemies. She is in the sunset, and somehow, she's in me.

This is beauty.

How do I get back to her?

Ultimately, beauty is a mindset you can learn and grow. Even though I felt pretty growing up, I also found myself being used a lot. People would only come to me because of how I looked, or for what they thought I could give them, verses because they wanted to know me or valued who I was. I used people, and they did the same to me. Every weekend, every school dance, all the girls would get ready together, and I would end up doing everyone's hair and makeup. I was invited to everyone's parties. I was in everyone's photos, but when I needed something from them, they never reciprocated. I felt like I worked so hard to make everyone else feel special, but once they achieved their goal, they didn't need me anymore.

When I was in eighth grade, one of the athletes at my school was talking to my best friend and I. This boy and my friend were both exceptional athletes. They spoke about the season's busy schedule and what areas of track they wanted to compete in. I, however, excelled at art, music, and creative extracurricular activities. When I didn't have anything to add to the conversation, this boy remarked, "Oh so you're only here to be pretty."

When my best friend didn't say anything in my defense, it really hurt me. She and I never had the same hobbies, but we didn't need that to build our friendship. We hung out all the time. We typically drove to school together and spent hours after school with each other. We told each other everything. She was my closest friend at the time. When this boy said that, however, I questioned why we were friends. I felt as though I didn't have anything valuable to add to my friendships. This simple conversation amplified my insecurity big time and confirmed what I felt other people thought of me. Because I did use beauty as a tool, other people saw me as that—a tool to be used. People only interacted with me because of how I made them look. People only interacted with the perception of who I was (because that's what I allowed them to access) rather than who I actually felt I was.

This really hit me when I got sick in highschool and was diagnosed with a nerve disease. I lost a ton of weight, control of muscle function, and ultimately ended up in hospice care for about two and a half years. I am fully recovered, happy, and healthy now, but at the time, I felt both mentally and physically unattractive. I was insecure, angry, and incredibly depressed. I was weak, super skinny, and hadn't seen the sun in who knows how long. I was losing control of my body and part of who I was. At that point, how I looked didn't matter. Because all my relationships were built on what I could do for other people, when I couldn't do anything, they stopped showing up.

To their credit, no teenager in their first year of highschool wants to spend their time watching someone wither away. I also hadn't invested deeply enough to keep them when things got hard. Alone in my room, I could see how part of that was my fault. I had to take responsibility. I hated the way I looked, even now when I get too skinny, or too pale, it reminds me of that season.

More than how I looked, however, I hated the way I had treated people. That was a big shift for me in a lot of ways. Having this realization changed how I used what I had and how I treated people.

When I was finally healthy enough to come back to school my senior year, I started building friendships that weren't centered around looks or what someone could do for me. I stopped caring what everyone thought on the outside and got to know people I wouldn't have given the time of day before. This allowed me to know people and be known on a deeper level. I wasn't trying to put on a show. I wasn't performing. This allowed me to truly be present.

I also started playing with beauty a lot. I cut all my hair off, changed the color about every month, and tried new styles constantly. I wasn't trying to impress people anymore. I was learning to love myself and wanted to express my personality. I had to shift the mindset of what beauty meant in me and what I found beautiful in people. My past actually set me up to be incredibly good at what I do now. I had to take responsibility for my own actions and thought processes, and figure out ways to walk in my beauty in a healthy way.

I read a lot of books. I asked questions to those around me about how to do things well. I also asked a lot of questions internally. Asking questions is important if you are going to uncover your true beautiful identity. Get to the root of what you even like.

These questions helped me pinpoint the source of my beauty:

- Who were you as a kid?
- What brought you the most joy?
- What brings you the most joy now?
- Are you fighting that?
- When were the times where you felt the most confident?

- Do you have the kinds of friends or relationships you want to have?
- Are you treating people in congruence with the type of person you want to be?
- Do you tell yourself the things you want to hear from other people?
- Are you waiting on another person to romance you and make you feel like you're worthy or beautiful?
- Are there adjustments in your answers to any of these questions that need to be made?

Take ownership of these things. Love and believe in yourself now. You being who you want to be is your responsibility. Ultimately, you feeling and knowing that you're beautiful is also your choice. You need to know and believe you are an amazing person. When someone else tells you they think you;re beautiful, it should be a wonderful compliment to receive, not a life altering moment you're depending on. When you let people dictate your identity, that's when you get stuck.

What people say to you should only be a compliment or an opinion. Their words shouldn't be a stake in the ground. They shouldn't have a hold over your life. Only you should have that.

That doesn't mean things people say will never hurt, but it does mean that it's your responsibility to heal from the hurt and move on. You are responsible for yourself. You are responsible for how you feel. When you hold that responsibility, that's when you begin to embody the beautiful person you are. That's also when you invite, and attract the compliments and things you crave and deserve instead of desperately chasing after them.

Beauty is a mindset.

The Bible talks about it, and every self help superstar loves to quote it: "You shall love your neighbor as yourself." (Matthew 22:39, NKJV)

But let's be honest. You're not really going to love people well if you don't first love yourself (that's why it says "as yourself"). It feels counterintuitive. So much of what is socially normal has said it's selfish to take care of yourself. "Self love" has only recently been a subject of focus, and even now, it's usually referred to as taking a night off to drink a glass of wine and have a nice bath.

Taking care of you actually puts the world around you at ease. Think about it this way, when you do really well at your job, you get a promotion. When you manage your money well, you get more of it. If this is true in these areas, how much more true is it for when you take good care of yourself?

You are worth way more than money or a title. This might be a hard concept to believe at first. You may not have viewed yourself this way before, or have had a healthy mindset around worth, but we'll work on that.

Beauty, confidence, and lifestyle are all a mindset. Your self worth, value, and the way you view yourself is all wrapped up in how you think. Because of this, *you will have to renew your thoughts and mind often*. Take time to recall the vision you had of yourself earlier, the picture you had of your "Most Beautiful Life." Now start talking to yourself as though you are already that version of yourself. When

thoughts contradict that view of yourself, stop. Don't listen
to them. Take a moment and affirm to yourself who you
really are and the journey you're on. That is a reset. Do it as
often as needed.

I have to do this almost constantly. The key to consistent
confidence in your beauty and self worth is constantly
reaffirming your truth, your security in your identity. Doing
this moves your worth and beauty from a feeling you only
experience here and there to a deep belief system and
mindset. Keep renewing your thoughts and redirecting your
self-talk until they align with a beauty mindset, until you can
say and believe "I am beautiful. I am worthy. Beauty is a part
of who I am." This might feel funny to say at first—maybe
even a little awkward or painful—but it is true. Even when
you forget your true identity, you can always bring yourself
back. The more often you do this, the easier it is to stay in it.
That's the difference between a thought of "I feel beautiful in
this moment," and a belief system of "I am beautiful."

Beauty itself is holistic in nature. It comes from a healthy
place and is expressed in layers. I have come to learn the
universal beauty rule is that beauty produces more beauty. If
you do not first love yourself, you won't build or attract the
things that you love. Beauty is an essence and a lifestyle, so
let it translate with all your heart, soul, and mind first.
Everything else will fall into place.

Questions from your Beauty Godmother

1.   *What are some affirmations you can say over yourself?*

Write out 3-5 affirmations that are great things about who you are or even who you want to be. Post these on your bathroom mirror to look at daily, or keep them in your purse for when you need a good reset

2.   *Who will be affected when you are being your most beautiful and confident self?*

Our growth and successes make a way for others to reach that same success. Our health feeds the relationships we have. Will your spouse or close friendships be more joyful and intimate because you are bringing the best version of yourself to them? Will a younger sibling, or child, or employee have a better set up for success because of your example?

Chapter 5
My Beauty Journey

I've talked about different times when a shift happened in my life, and I chose to not care what others thought of me. There were other times, in my lowest points, where I realized how I had mishandled myself and the people around me. It's been a long journey coming from a mindset where beauty was superficial, sexual, and a tool to use to where I'm at now. There's not a single pinpointed moment where I suddenly began to think about beauty as a healthy lifestyle. The inner confidence I now have in who I am, and my desire to help other people discover theirs as well has been a process.

I started taking back my control with an out of the box style and edgy fashion sense. I baby stepped into having honest, vulnerable conversations with my friends about who I was and how I wanted to be treated. Even after all of my hardship and growth, beauty was still a struggle. I was no longer using beauty as a way to manipulate people, but there were still times where I felt insecure and afraid to let people really see me. I remember the first time I wore no makeup to school. I cried because I felt so ashamed of my skin. Part of me still thought I somehow was not valuable if I didn't look a certain way. Growing up in the 90's and early 2000's, the "natural" look was not in. It was thin eyebrows, sultry smokey eyes, defined cheekbones, and being super skinny. I still love a lot of that style, but as a kid, I began to tie my confidence into how well I could do my makeup, not how my face actually looked.

I also struggled with acne for most of my life which threw another wrench into the whole getting ready routine. I remember in one of my high school health classes, they talked about how different things, including wearing heavy makeup (which I wore every day) contributed to acne. It could have been the "Just say no to drugs" posters in the room, but I remember thinking, "Oh my gosh, am I addicted to makeup?!" It was hilarious, but it worked. The next day, I quit makeup cold turkey for a week. Even more ironic was how many boys at school complimented me for not wearing makeup! Over time, insecurity around makeup and my skin began to fall away, and grew confident with or without it. Makeup became neutral. The desire to wear it wasn't bad, and the decision to not wear it no longer evoked negative feelings.

There were several key areas of my life that needed to shift before I could really start to embody the beauty I'd come to realize was within myself.

Forming Relationships With Other Beautiful Women

I needed to get around beautiful women, and I mean truly beautiful women who weren't just gorgeous on the outside, but who owned their story, and wanted me to succeed in life as well. Women I could look up to, women I could ask questions and process with. When I meet someone who is living beautifully and authentically in spite of their trauma, I ask them how they accomplished this. I encourage you to do this as well. People who are truly healed or really successful in any area want other people to receive that same healing and success. If they are defensive or feel too insecure to share, they're probably not as healed or successful as they're projecting. Gatekeeping is a huge signpost for insecurity or overcompensating for a deficit in another area. Don't take someone's decline to share with you personally, move on to people who are open and excited about getting you your success.

I started doing this a lot when I left the dark lifestyle of witchcraft because the reality was, I did not know how to live a normal life. I had to relearn so much—how to think, how to interact with people, how I saw myself. It was like living in a new country where you didn't know a lot of the culture or language. It took some getting used to, but I just started asking a lot of questions, and allowed myself to try new things.

There were a few years when my mom left, and I became a partial guardian to my younger sisters. I was about 18 and had no idea what I was doing. There was a beautiful, wonderful woman I knew at my church named Stacy, who looked way too young to have six kids of her own (but she did). This woman took me in and taught me everything, from how to feed a family on a budget, to how to pay bills, to how to register everyone at school or the doctors office. She also helped me process my emotions during that time and taught me how to have a nurturing mindset (essentially mothering) and how to put others' needs first while not diminishing who

I was as a person. She taught me a lot about strength, but she also taught me a lot about communicating with vulnerability and being caring as a woman—parts of beauty I had not yet had the privilege to internalize. I needed someone who would let me ask questions without doing everything for me. Stacy was very much the stable part of my life during that season. Life has since changed, and we now live in different states, but Stacy has always continued to be a great friend.

Another woman who has believed in me, oftentimes more than I believed in myself, is Fiona. I also met her through church. She has a bold, fiery personality that instantly drew me to her, but she was also so encouraging, friendly, and extremely generous. One time in particular, she mentioned having a tumultuous upbringing with her mom. Despite that, she had learned to forgive her and have a healthy relationship. This had been years after my mom left, and when Fiona told this story, I realized I wasn't ready to forgive just yet, let alone open the door to a relationship with her. I wanted to know more about her journey and how she got to that place.

I learned there was a lot of trauma from her past that she didn't allow to weigh down her present circumstances. Since that conversation, Fiona has been a substantial part of my life. She really taught me how to move from a mindset of just surviving through life, to really thriving in it. She played a huge part in getting me to bridge the gap in the relationship with my own mom. She also encouraged me to start my own business as well as helped walk me through the whole process. Fiona has helped me fight through and celebrate so many things in my life. Anytime I have had a goal or a dream, she would help me see it, create a plan to get there, and then become my biggest supporter along the way. Fiona taught me that beauty has so much more to do with your heart, than it does with looking fabulous (which she does). She also encouraged and allowed me to always pursue the best version of myself. She has changed my life in innumerable ways, and for that I am eternally grateful.

These women, among many others, showed me not only how to achieve the goals and lifestyle I wanted for myself, but how to do it well and how to do it beautifully. When you see something you want in another woman, don't get jealous. Ask questions! Invite them out to coffee. Allow them to share their story, and then actually do what they recommend! That last part is the biggest thing. It may or may not work for you, but if you don't at least try to implement what they shared with you, it's a waste of both your time. You don't need to idolize or copy everything they do, but when you open yourself up to learn from other women, you expand yourself to their resources and wisdom. In doing this, you also expand the boundaries of your life. You begin to attract more solutions and people who want to help you, or cheer you on as you succeed.

Taking Care of My Physical Health

As I've grown, I have found that taking care of myself holistically has brought me the most joy, the most love, and the most beauty. We can disconnect ourselves from our own body. Even using the word "body" can sound lifeless, like it's being used as a scientific term in a text book and doesn't have a mind. Yet you would be amazed at how much more of you will come alive when you become intune with, and nurture, the body that you have.

Your body is not just your limbs or something to put clothes on when you get ready. Your body is what interacts with the physical world. It takes in the sun and the breeze. It holds onto trauma. It processes food and gives you energy. It's the literal thing that will carry you to the vision you have of your best self. Your body can change and will grow with you, so begin to show it some love. Health goals look different for everyone, but across the board, taking care of your body is a must. Good, nutritious food and consistently exercising have a positive effect on your mood, mental clarity, energy, and immune system—not to mention these things help your body to look and physically feel good to be in. I started really working out, cleaning up my eating, and resting well because I didn't like that my body felt more like a burden than an asset through my normal work day. I am a much nicer, productive person when I'm taking care of my body.

Cultivating Healthy Mindsets

I can talk endlessly about your mindset. What you believe is possible is truly the blueprint for your life. Mindset is also something that changes and grows with you. How you think about yourself matters. Do not be disconnected from your mind. Think about what you're thinking about. If the thought is not serving you, don't dwell on it. Get in the habit of only watching and hearing uplifting things. *Preoccupy your mind with the good.* There was a season where I had sticky notes everywhere! My bathroom mirror, my bedroom, my car, and my school binder were all filled with reminders of what to focus on—positive quotes, affirmations, whatever stuck out to me that I felt I needed in front of me as much as possible. I still practice this when I need to get out of a mental funk. I'll put reminders on my phone, change the background, or only listen to certain playlists until I really begin to adopt the mindsets I wanted to have.

Building Healthy Relationships

Relationships are another area of health that can have a huge impact on your life. Not everyone is going to be your best friend, and that's okay. You should be looking for mutually beneficial relationships with people you can also believe in and serve. You can support and encourage each other to keep moving towards being your best selves. These are people you can be honest with, people who are safe to go through a bad day with but who will also celebrate the great days with you. Don't be afraid to evaluate and work on the relationships you have with the people closest to you. Part of your beauty and health is how you get to interact with and impact the people around you.

Acknowledging issues that have come up in my physical health, mindsets, or relationship has allowed me to make necessary adjustments so I can heal. The process of healing wasn't as painful as ignoring the problem or trying to overcompensate in another area to cover it. Allowing myself to process the hurts that come up, and celebrate the parts of me that are flourishing, is an everyday thing I have come to love. Sometimes you have to be really honest with yourself. Process where those mindsets came from, release it, and flood your whole world with a shift in your perspective until it becomes your new belief.

Get in the habit of always looking for the beauty in each season and situation. I'm not saying every situation is good, but there can be good in it.

I've felt betrayed and wronged. My mom leaving was a big one, but as I began to forgive, I started to have compassion. It didn't make the situation any less wrong, but there was beauty in the woman it developed me into. Eventually there was even depth in the relationship we began to cultivate.

Realize that every situation is temporary, and your whole life is not one event. Constantly reminding yourself of what you are grateful for can help you not drown in a negative circumstance. Having stable, positive people who are pushing you towards your best self in every season, keeping you encouraged in low times and integrous in high times, is also extremely important. Vent, process, journal, but decide to stay true to yourself at the end of a bad day. Celebrate the good things, and don't lose your honor or integrity when celebrating. You may need to adjust how you push to be your best self in each season, but be pushing for it nonetheless. There is beauty in growth and depth in overcoming obstacles or pain. I'm confident that every season can be beautiful— that who I am, and the woman I am becoming, is someone I can be proud of. I believe this is the same for you.

Questions from your Beauty Godmother

*1.   What is something you will do to nurture or take
      care of your body?*

These could be in things in your eating, exercise, or even
resting habits.

*2.   What is something you will do to feed healthy
      mindsets?*

These could be things like cleaning up what you listen to,
creating a habit of affirmations, and spending less time in
front of a screen.

*3.   What is something you will do to strengthen your
      relationships?*

These could be things like creating intentional time with
people, creating opportunities to listen to and serve those
around you, or even starting new friendships and reaching
out to new people who have a successful area of life that you
want to emulate.

Chapter 6
The Laws of Beauty

Beauty means something different to everyone. My goal is to empower you to identify and express your beauty in a healthy and edifying way. There are certain elements to beauty that make it what it is—fundamental truths, or laws, that when absent turn beauty into a superficial trend that's image based. I want to get to the strong, foundational core of beauty and build from there. These are the five "laws" I've uncovered that will help you test whether something is carrying true beauty or not.

1. You work from a place of beauty, not toward beauty

You start with beauty. You are beautiful. Period.

You are made that way. It's part of who you are. Everything physical is just an accessory to the beauty that is in you. The inherent beauty within the feminine spirit is the most needed, and the most misunderstood, part of us. A lot of us were told, or taught, beauty was solely based on attractiveness, so we spent our whole lives trying to be sexually appealing. We performed because we thought beauty was only about being visually stimulating. To think you are an image, or that the only thing you have to offer is a performance, disconnects you from the depth of who you are. It's like trying to capture the immersive experience of a vacation to a new country—the sights, sounds, culture, landscape, and attractions—through a simple pencil drawing.

Don't try to put all your value in a one dimensional representation of yourself that will end up limiting you. One dimensional things are superficial. They are objects. There's no depth to them other than what is seen on the surface. They have no life on them. You were not designed to be one dimensional or an object. You are a multi-faceted person.

When the deeper, very complex part of you is mismanaged, it becomes fragmented.

You don't just need this year's current beauty standard or the next season's fashion do's and don'ts. You need the love for yourself, the beauty that comes from deep friendship, and a healthy community. You need people cheering you on who are also a safe place to run to when times are hard. You need the peace beauty offers. You need to be inspired and encouraged. Safety, softness, and strength—these makeup the beautiful spirit.

People contain unfathomable variety. You should view people with that same frame of mind you would have when visiting an unfamiliar country, for there are worlds inside us. Again, the beauty in you is a very deep thing, and the world around you needs the world inside you. You may have been beat down, discouraged, or feel lost on how to express that beauty, but it is in you and yours to express.

Practice telling yourself you are beautiful before you get out of bed. Before you even look in the mirror, get dressed up and take a really good selfie. Before you attack your to-do list, take time to be grateful for your life, your journey, and the new day. This might be uncomfortable for you at first, but I want you to literally say out loud, "I am beautiful."

Your being responds to what you say. Your mind, and even your body, will begin to act in accordance with what you declare over yourself. If you say you're ugly, your entire being positions itself to follow that sentence and will eventually begin to reject opportunities to be, feel, or even see itself as attractive. You may even begin to hide, and feel uncomfortable being complimented.

When you call yourself beautiful, your mind and body run in that direction. Naturally, you'll begin to emanate this. Your posture becomes open and confident, and you begin to attract other beautiful things because your being believes it belongs in a beautiful state. So say it.

Once you do that, take note of how you feel.

Do this *especially* if you don't yet believe in your own beauty. Being beautiful is just that, a state of *being*. I want you to get used to the idea that you *do not* have to work to be beautiful. It's something you are. When you come from a place appreciating yourself, your body, your personality, and your mind, every other beautiful thing you want to do or be a part of comes much easier.

2. Beauty is good

"Every experience of beauty points to eternity."
-Hans Urs von Balthasar

I believe the world is inherently good. Yes, there is a lot of chaos and evil, but at their origin, people and the world are good. Beauty is also good.

Truly beautiful things give life. The ocean with all of its plants, animals, and the whole colorful world below the surface is full of life. Even looking at a garden— producing food, bees pollinating the plants, the plants cleaning the air— you can see a whole, beautiful life-giving ecosystem. When you look in nature, the things we find beautiful feed into these life-giving ecosystems.

A mother birthing a child is another example of this. Pregnancy and giving birth is the epitome of *giving life*. I understand there are certain negative narratives around pregnancy and birth in this day and age. Oftentimes culture at large likes to portray pregnancy and children as something that is inconvenient for women—unless she *really* wants to have a baby. I would encourage you to question where that narrative came from. Your body has the ability to create another human. That alone speaks to a deeper part of us. We bring life. Every mother I talk to is amazed her body created life. Birth is life changing, and the result is another person. I've heard countless mothers express, "I never knew I could love something or someone that much," after having their first child. There's just no words for it. Beauty is in many ways unexplainably good.

Another author, Staci Eldridge, made the point in her book, *Captivating,* that on a practical level, there is no reason for sunsets to be as beautiful as they are. They are just a simple change from day to night, one hour to the next. However, they are one of the most stunning sites that, if the weather is good, we can enjoy everyday. Sunsets stop us in our tracks every time. People take pictures or make paintings to capture the scene in the sky. It's a simple thing, but a thing that brings hope back into your focus. Color and newness sparks another breath of life into you. This is you when you are in your natural and good state.

We need experiences like this. We need beauty. Just like food feeds the body, beauty nourishes our soul. Being in your favorite place relaxes you, somehow puts you back together. Interior decorators will design layouts and spaces for employees to be around art and a window with a view so they can have better workflow and productivity.

We put so much effort, money and design into making sure our atmospheres speak of our taste. We long to be surrounded by and immersed in beautiful things. It makes you feel like you can breathe again. It reminds you that this is how life should be. These things affect us this way because beauty is good for us.

It's sometimes messy, and not over the counter clean, but beauty really is in all the moments of life we call good. We consider an act of heroism to be beautiful. We cry with joy in response to the vows at a wedding. We are inspired by the sacrifice a parent gives to better their child's life.

Beauty is good, and you should surround yourself with it often.

Beauty is good, and it is okay to be beautiful.

The beauty in you is a good thing. You are beautiful, and your desire to be beautiful, to be desired, and to create more beauty is natural. It's how you as a woman connect with the world. In the same way we expect strength from a man, the world longs to experience beauty from a woman. Most of our shame comes from feeling we have failed in this core part of our identity. At some point, you've probably felt that sinking gut punch when you offered your beauty, your true self in any situation—with your relationships, or even creative input—and nothing happened. It changed nothing. Maybe the thought has run through your mind, "I made no difference, and therefore I am of no significance." Even heavier pain comes from being not only unaccepted but also feeling rejected.

When hurt with the matter of beauty, women are struck to their core because it has so much significance in who we are. It's how we express ourselves. However, just because someone else may have misused your beauty, doesn't dampen the principle of beauty as a whole. You are allowed to put that situation, that thought process, in a different place in your life. It may have been a very real, very painful part of your story, but it is also just that—part of the story. The hurt and rejection are not your identity. Don't let one part of the story rob you of the good. Don't let it cheat you out of the powerful beauty inside you. Those people were not acting within their true beauty. When people act out of character, or outside of true beauty, it has way more to do with them and their own insecurity, than it does with you. You are beautiful. You are allowed to be beautiful, and your beauty is a very good thing.

3. Beauty is not perfect

When looking up the word "perfect" on Google, this is what I found:

1. Having all the required or desirable elements, qualities or characteristics.
2. Conforming absolutely to the description or definition of an ideal type.
3. Absolute beyond improvement.
4. Being entirely without fault or defect.

A drive for excellence is one thing. Excellence pushes us to produce and perform at our best. A perfection complex, however, is constricting and harmful. Words like "conforming," "absolute," and "faultless" actually kill creativity, especially when it comes to your expression of beauty.

Think about it this way. Imagine if I asked you to draw a perfect circle without access to specialized tools. Most people's idea of a perfect circle is a computer generated circle, completely even and equal in circumference without any gap, blemish, or inconsistency all the way around. It's next to impossible to produce a perfect circle by hand with no tools or edits.

Now, a more personal question: Do you have this same dictionary definition for perfect, this same computer generated standard towards your self image? Image—there's another taboo word. Image is how others view you. Your representation of your external form, the impression you present.

We have the tools, the edits, and the resources accessible to change how we look in any picture. We have gotten very good at presenting and posing, not only in pictures but also as a lifestyle. I'm not talking about work requirements or appropriate social conduct. I'm talking about adopting certain cultural beliefs about how you present yourself and live your life. There is a prevailing perfection mindset that you have to live or look a certain way to be happy and loved, and it's a lie. Beauty does not fit into perfected molds.

Let's use fashion models as an example. To be good at what they do, a high end model will change their hair color, hair length, muscle tonality, posture, and even weight. They are trained to present their best features while allowing things less flattering to fall back. They understand angles, lighting, and camera interaction. They can smile in any weather, keep their eyes from squinting or tearing against blaring studio lights or the sun, and hold awkward positions for any given length of time (or at least in the time it takes to get the right photo). They're even trained in the discipline of special breathing techniques.

Needless to say, posing as a profession is tiring; living a life full of posing, even more so. Are you contorting yourself? Are you positioning instead of being? Are you afraid to share something as common and as natural as a blemish?

You are not meant to conform yourself out of having a personality. The astringent, computer generated, flawlessly curated definition of the perfect woman cannot move, or breathe, or live. As soon as she does, she is no longer that standard of perfection.

Can I invite you to let go of that excruciatingly unnecessary pressure, and offer you a different view? Maybe what makes the circle perfect, is the fact that you completed it? You've connected it all the way through, and you didn't let any inconsistencies or gaps stop you. Wholeness. You gave it your all, allowing yourself to be complete in and of yourself with all the mess, the stand out details, and the journey of improvements. The living and the realness give validation to the image represented. That is what is beautiful.

That is what makes you perfect.

4. Beauty is Healing

Think about why you give sick or grieving people flowers. The flowers don't fix the situation. They don't make the person any less sick, or less sad, but the beauty of those flowers has a healing quality. Beauty heals us. Its comfort reminds us life can and will be better. It brings us hope.

One of the best conversations I've ever had was with my Nana after she expressed to me that she needed some alone time. This initially hurt my feelings a little bit. I wanted to spend time with her. I also didn't know where she was coming from emotionally, so I called her one night to understand her perspective and make sure she was alright.

We talked for an hour. She expressed some really hard things about her previous divorce, how other family members handled it, and how that made her feel unimportant—like her feelings about the situation didn't matter. It broke my heart to hear she felt alone and unsupported. I shared some really vulnerable things around times when I felt rejected and not prioritized in my parents divorce. We got to connect through the realness of pain and loss in life, but also offer each other solutions and the presence of our support.

I think this was the first time my Nana acknowledged some of the hurt and disappointment in her life, at least out loud. I knew about her story, our family history, and where we had come from, but it was so different to hear some of these things from her perspective, how it felt to live through her life. I always loved and respected my Nana, but when I had the courage to ask certain questions, and she had the vulnerability to answer them, I gained new insight into why my Nana was as amazing as she was.

She loved her family. She always sacrificed for them and put them first. However, after years and decades of only being a good sister, a good wife, a good mom, and eventually, a good grandmother, she never prioritized herself.

She expressed how in a lot of ways, she had lived her life playing a role for others and forgot what she liked. Her desire for alone time wasn't because she was mad at us or didn't want to be around us. She just wanted to get back to the place where she loved herself again and was at her most healthy. When we had this conversation, I tried to give her permission to be herself. It may not sound like a big deal, especially from a granddaughter, but I think that may have been the first time (at least the first time in a long time) someone freed her and championed her to be herself.

It's amazing what happens when people come together with the intention of only giving to each other. You feel freed and supported. You build a two way street and a flow is formed. It's always a blessing to talk to my Nana because she is such an inspiration to me. Only wisdom, insight, and support are being poured into the relationship, so only those things can be picked up. In that kind of environment, you are safe to share your pain. You are freed to receive your healing. Beauty is just present and engaged with what is needed now. Beauty isn't the person who doesn't walk through anything. We've *all* walked through something no matter how big or small. Beauty is the person who walked through hell, but still decided to smile and carry heaven anyway.

5.Beauty produces beauty

"For attractive lips, speak words of kindness.
For lovely eyes, seek out the good in people.
For a slim figure, share your food with the hungry.
For beautiful hair, let a child run their fingers through it once a day.
For poise, walk with the knowledge that you never walk alone."
- Sam Levenson

You probably have experienced the pretty girl with the rotten heart—the beauty guru at the makeup store who sucks you in, steals all your money, and makes you feel even worse about yourself after the encounter. Then there is the endless, mindless media content that is impossibly perfect, plastic, and designed to make you jealous. Those dreadful experiences have a different motive and are not real beauty. All of those situations are really just greed, insecurity, or someone else's fear hijacking a pretty face.

Anything truly beautiful leaves a mark of more beauty. You feel excited and confident after being in the presence of someone who walks in their beauty. Truly beautiful women are loving. They are kind. They are strong, but also gentle and nurturing. They don't need to degrade anyone to lift themselves up. Beauty is shared and developed.

It is heart breaking to me to see what some extreme feminists have become. I'm all about female empowerment, equal opportunity, and celebrating the feminine spirit. That's the whole purpose of this book. However, becoming harshly competitive against other women, tearing down the male species, or labeling masculinity as toxic, is not lifting humankind up.

There will be experiences that are hurtful, and unfair. Healing from that part of your story is necessary, keeping a strong yet soft, beautiful, and kind heart is imperative.

The reality is that unresolved trauma doesn't just go away—it grows. It may not be aggressive now, but an unhealed part of you will eventually limit your ability to receive good things. A part of you that is still resentful, hurt, or bitter can begin to form negative filters on the way you see the world. When things are allowed to trigger you and begin to draw you into a defensive posture, your ability to connect in healthy relationships becomes inhibited. Oppositely, a woman who has not only survived her history, but who has also done the work to heal, is the most free to love and live at the capacity she wants to.

We need to teach differently. We need to raise the next generation better, starting with conversations and creating resources to educate and lift each other up. If we become bitter, or problem-minded instead of solution-minded, we aren't acting in alignment with our true beautiful identity. We stop working from a place of victory.

What is truly beautiful will multiply, give, and produce more beauty. Just like a flower's seed will produce more of the same flower, beautiful things grow more beauty.

* * *

These principles will help you build a strong foundation, as well as reinforce your confidence in your journey with beauty. How you express beauty will be personally and uniquely yours. Take your time to process and work through each law. Think through how they make sense in your life and how to best begin implementing them in the way that expresses your own beauty. Know you are beautiful. It is embedded in who you are. You are not working to become beautiful, you are working to pull that beauty out and into everything you do.

Remember the goodness true beauty carries and that you do not need to settle for counterfeit or negative-feeling versions of beauty. Beauty is good, and it's okay to be beautiful. The world needs the beauty you bring.

Beauty does not need to be picture perfect, but rather authentic and real. When you bring your best (your full) self, you turn a one dimensional image of beauty into a life giving expression and lifestyle. Let go of the pressure of perfection and celebrate the journey of progressing.

If you need healing around beauty, that's okay. In fact, healing and beauty often go hand in hand. Healing releases the opportunity for more beauty and wholeness. Beauty itself can also be a very healing thing. It's a nourishing power and resource.

Anything truly beautiful will produce and create even more beauty.

Don't hesitate to surround yourself with beauty and lots of it. Reach out to women you admire and ask them about it. Create a community with women who are excited about healing, loving, and encouraging themselves and others. Listen to positive voices, music, and media.

If you live this way, beauty won't be just an attribute. It will become something you embody.

Questions from your Beauty Godmother

1. *What is a way that you can surround yourself with more beauty, more often?*

This can be adding artwork that speaks to you in your workplace, taking fifteen minutes out of your day to sit in nature, or even wearing clothes that make you feel pretty and confident more often.

2. *If true beauty is authentic and real, what are some ways you can share your vulnerability, and genuine self to make beauty whole?*

This can be opening up to a friend and sharing something more personal that you haven't with them yet, letting people in on how you are doing, asking others how they are really doing, or even intentionally journaling daily.

3. *You may have experienced competitive, comparing, or even tearing down interactions with other women. What is a way you can begin to encourage, uplift and support the beauty in others, ensuring that the beauty in you produces that in others as well?*

This can be as simple as making it a point to intentionally compliment as many people as you can throughout the day (you would be amazed at how positively most people respond), or even just sitting down with a friend and really telling them how proud you are of them and encouraging them.

Chapter 7
The Magic of Haircare

It's time to talk about how your soul translates to the beauty you carry on the outside. Although I do believe that real beauty is not a superficial thing, I would not be telling you the truth if I didn't address the part of beauty that is physical. Part of beauty does deal with the tangible and has to do with your outside image. However, this does not change how we approach beauty. Once you have a healthy, loving mindset towards yourself, other people, and beauty, that mindset can carry over into how you take care of your physical being. You can now love, celebrate, and nurture your body, its health, and physical beauty. We are removing the lie that beauty is only skin deep and replacing it with the truth that what you present to the world is an extension of the beauty *within* you.

Everyone has totally different styles—some people are more sporty, some are more casual, and others like more glam. What you like goes beyond what trend you pick. It communicates style, and style goes deeper than fashion. Style communicates a way of life. It communicates how you want to be approached.

Style isn't everything. You don't want to be judged based on your looks, but the way you look can invite and affect how the world perceives and receives you. How you care for your outside image can determine if other people want to get to know what's on the inside. Our goal is to allow the essence of your inner, inherent beauty to also penetrate your physical appearance.

You can have a great heart and be the sweetest person, but on the outside, if you don't take care of yourself, it alludes to the inner chaos that's still inside of you. You're out of alignment. When people see you, they won't assume you have your life together. Perception shifts when people see you take care of yourself. When you have a certain aesthetic, it does open the door for more opportunities. Outside of that, physically taking care of yourself shows you value yourself. It reflects an inner confidence and therefore demonstrates that you will value other people at the same level. When you physically represent how much you value yourself, people instinctively assume you'll value them more as well.

In this chapter, we're specifically going to dive into how to best take care of your hair so you can reflect your inner identity on the outside. Hair is an extension of your identity, partly because it's actually attached to you, but also because it makes up 80% of your selfie. And *it is* something you actually have to take care of. There's health and hygiene involved.

Hair is different from makeup (which we will also be talking about later). Some of us like makeup, and some of us don't. Even those of us who do like makeup have no makeup days, which is completely normal. This is not the case with hair. If you don't do your hair for 6 months, you *look like* someone who hasn't taken care of themselves in 6 months. You look unkempt.

If you've ever wondered how to best take care of your hair, keep reading. We'll go over everything from how to nurture your hair to basic styling techniques so you can look and most importantly *feel* like the best version of you.

Note: throughout the next two chapters, you'll be seeing words that have an asterisks * in front of them. I've put these words in a glossary at the end of the book if you feel like you need more explanation as to what they mean.

Feed your hair

Get what you need. Care for your hair well.

Make sure your hair, skin, and nails are getting the right nutrients. Drink lots of water, eat healthy foods, and take vitamins. I have a lot of clients who love adding collagen protein powder to their daily coffee or smoothies. Collagen in general is a great supplement to add to your beauty routine, but it's especially good if you're trying to grow longer or fuller hair!

Some things to add to your diet could be:

- Vitamins: A, B (Biotin is a type of B vitamin), and C. These are crucial for cell growth and creating a healthy set up for hair to be built and then grow within the follicle. Your hair and skin need antioxidants to help protect from damage or stress, and amino acids to build the proteins necessary to actually make hair. Omega 3's and fatty acids have also been linked to stimulating the growth phase of hair, and its thickness. Deficiency in any of these can affect your hair's health and growth.

- Collagen: This is a protein your body naturally produces. It is responsible for slowing down aging, like graying hair and wrinkles in the skin, and helps create the building blocks needed for producing hair. Adding this after the age 25 can help prevent signs of aging, hair loss, and promote hair regrowth and thickening.

Please note that different amounts of vitamins and supplements affect people differently. You should consult with your doctor for what you should add to your routine.

There are amazing services and treatments salons offer to rejuvenate your hair. However, any good stylist will tell you that doing what you can at home to maintain your hair's health makes a world of difference for how your hair looks and feels, not to mention the state of your bank account. It's actually much easier, better for you, and for your stylist, to schedule little hair check-up appointments to maintain your hair's luxurious look and feel, rather than bringing it back from the dead every appointment.

Keep the basics of washing

1) Shampoo:

What may not be common knowledge is that shampoo was made predominantly for your scalp, not your hair. It's made to remove build up from product and naturally produced oils or sweat off of the hair follicle. This gives your hair room to breathe and grow.

To *correctly* wash your hair with shampoo, spend a little time getting the scalp and hair fully saturated with water before adding any of the product. This will help activate and spread the shampoo once it is introduced.

Concentrate on the scalp and roots of the hair when shampooing. A common mistake is thinking that picking all of your hair up on top of your head and then swishing and massaging it around like a washing machine is the correct way to wash your hair. The shampoo commercials lied; this is not correct. Scrubbing your ends like that is probably adding more damage.

When washing, leave the hair down. Massage the shampoo into your scalp and root area. As you rinse it out, *the shampoo running down your hair's strand is actually enough to gently cleanse the ends without damaging them.* Repeat this process as many times as you feel necessary (especially if you have thicker or coarser hair), until product build up and/or odor is gone.

It is not uncommon to wash your hair two or three times in the shower.

Read the instructions on your shampoo bottle to see what the brand recommends for that particular product. At most, you should be washing your hair every other day, and at the least, once every ten days.

If you have thick, coarser, or ethnic hair and decide to go longer than ten days, I would recommend co-washing the hair in between shampoos. There are specific co-wash products, but you can also use a conditioner. The purpose of this is to remove product build up on the hair while maintaining moisture in the hair curl. The coarser the hair, the more moisture it will need. Using less striping shampoos, shampooing less often, and adding more conditioning (or a co-wash) will help the hair feel softer and more manageable.

A good way to test if you should wash your hair or not is to check for the presence of odor. You can also gently scratch your scalp. If you have any kind of build up under your nail after scratching, it's a good sign to wash your hair.

2) Conditioner:

Unlike shampoo, conditioner was made for your hair and your hair's ends. Your roots have the most access to the needed nutrients and oils. Coating your hair from scalp to end with conditioner may be adding to the build up on the scalp. It can cause your roots to get much more oily much faster, and may also disrupt your scalp's natural oil production pattern, causing a loss of volume in the root area.

Note that any type of product buildup can begin to clog the scalp and slow down hair growth.

Conditioner is made to detangle, smooth out, and moisturize the hair ends (they usually need the extra moisture).

In the shower, condition your ends only, starting from about the pony-tail and move down to ends. Leave it on for about 3-5 minutes, or whatever time is recommended on the product label, then rinse.

The type of product you use matters!

Use professional shampoo and conditioner! You need to buy these products from a salon or directly from the brand itself. There is a reason you have to be a certified beauty professional to have access to these products. When made, they use the highest grade of ingredients. Beauty professionals have education and training on which ingredients your specific hair type needs and can therefore partner with these product brands in using and selling them properly.

A salon is oftentimes required to go through preliminary coaching before they can carry a brand.

Outside of salons or licensed hair stylists, professional grade beauty brands have contracts with the supply stores. They do not sell to grocery stores or general public stores. If you see something you think is a high end product, or something you have seen at a salon in a grocery store, it is not that product. Stealing shipments and then diluting them or holding them until expired before selling to an uncertified store is unfortunately a common practice.

Non-professional brands (the ones not sold in salons) have poor quality ingredients that are often watered down, cheap, and include fillers, waxes, and detergents. Nine times out of ten, the reasons for scalp irritation, dandruff, overdrying, or greasy hair comes from using a poor quality shampoo or conditioner. If it is at the grocery store, you don't want it.

How to know which shampoo and conditioner to buy

- Fine to thinner hair: Generally, you should reach for a volumizing pair—something that isn't overly moisturizing or feels really thick or mayo-like to the touch. These can weigh the hair down.

- Thicker coarser hair: You may want to lean more towards smoothing shampoos and heavier conditioners. Use products with more hydration if needed.

- Curly hair: Your hair needs more moisture than you think it does. The more moisture a curl has, the more defined and smooth it will be. *When curls are lacking moisture, they begin to separate and frizz*, almost like little branches reaching out for as much moisture as they can get.

- If you're blonde: You may want to use a purple shampoo. *This is only for blondes who want to remove warmth.* If you like your blonde on the golden, sunkissed side, do not use this. Purple shampoo is a clarifying shampoo. Its goal is to clarify free radicals and elements that create a warmer, brassy tone on the blonde hair's surface. This means it can also dry out the hair, so you should not use it for every wash. If you want a *cool toned, platinum look, use a purple shampoo every other wash when you notice brassy tones popping up in your hair. Always follow up with a more moisturizing conditioner after using.

- Clarifying or medicinal shampoos: You should only use these as directed or for short periods of time. Typically, they are used in the salon as part of a treatment. At home, a clarifying treatment can be used on hair that has been overexposed to chlorinated water, feels gummy, or has an unnatural tint to it. It can help with removing a direct dye, like those crazy bright temporary hair colors, or the green tint that comes from being in the pool too much.

A clarifying shampoo is good to have on hand if you're in chlorinated water often or if you have little kids. They get into everything, and it's a good just in case product. A deep conditioner is recommended immediately after using any kind of clarifying shampoo.

- If you have lice or dandruff: Tea tree shampoo is a great treatment. It is also really *astringent and not recommended for an overly irritated, inflamed scalp, or a scalp with sores. It can be used to help fix a problem area like dandruff or non inflamed breakouts, but use should be discontinued as soon as the problem is alleviated. If the issue is lice, I would highly recommend seeking out professional help as well.

- Color protection: If you are coloring your hair in any way (blonding, darkening, covering gray), you should be using a shampoo and conditioner with a color preserving or protecting element. Typically, the product will list "color safe" somewhere on the label.

- Color depositing: These are made in shampoo and
  conditioner forms and are typically used to help keep
  *fashion tones for a longer time. If you plan on
  having a fashion tone like this in your hair for a long
  period of time, I highly recommend making this kind
  of shampoo or conditioner part of your regimen.
  They can also be used to enhance naturally produced
  colors, bringing a vibrancy to natural redheads, or
  adding depth to brunettes who feel a little dull. Please
  note that these color depositing shampoos and
  conditioners do not replace salon grade toners or
  hair color services. They are temporary enhancers
  and will likely completely leave the hair in one to two
  washes (which is great for kids or when you are
  experimenting with non-committal colors). They do
  leave a film on the hair and can stain your nails,
  shower, or pillow case.

Important Note: This is just a general guide, please
discuss this topic with your hairstylist, as they will know
much more about your hair's individual needs and the goals
you have for your hair.

Add deep conditioners here and there.

Deep conditioners are intense treatments that are
different from daily conditioners. They are concentrated and
designed to deposit specific nutrients in a short amount of
time. They can range from a little pick me up for some added
moisture and *shine, to the emergency response team
coming in to revive your hair's life. They are typically used
anywhere from once every couple of months to once every
other week. If you notice your hair feels extremely dry, even
with good shampoo and conditioner, adding a moisturizing

deep conditioner may be good to incorporate in your routine.

Use the right deep conditioner for the job.

Putting the wrong one on your hair, or using too much of the right one, could cause even more damage. Dry, brittle, and limp hair, for example, may need a treatment that adds a lot of strength and protein. However, if that same hair isn't given the time to recover and absorb all the newly introduced nutrients, the over-saturation may over-protienize* the hair, causing it to not fully absorb. All of that deep conditioner will be left just sitting on top of the hair. This can cause a not-so-pretty hardened shell layer to form over the hair and in most cases, will become more susceptible to damage.

Always read the product's purpose and consult with your hair professional about how to use it .

Coconut oil is a really good, natural, cost effective treatment. It helps retain the hair's protein and moisture. It's also an antifungal and has soothing qualities, which can help with dandruff or scalp irritation.

To use this as a treatment, coat the hair liberally from scalp to ends. Let the oil sit for at least 30 minutes, then wash it out with shampoo. DO NOT go out into the sun with coconut oil in your hair. Coconut oil is also a cooking agent, meaning that when it heats up it can actually begin to damage, or "cook," your hair.

Get trims religiously

A trim does not mean a full-on style change haircut. Regular trimming actually promotes the hair's healthy growth and keeps things balanced and polished looking.

Don't ignore split ends in an attempt to grow it out.

Have you ever spent months on end avoiding trims, trying to let your hair grow, only to realize it wasn't growing at all? Hair grows from the roots (if you color your hair regularly you know this very well).

Damage, however, usually starts at the ends.

What you may not know is that damage, whether it's dryness, split ends, or weak brittle hair, actually spreads. Split ends start as a fracture or "split" in the hair's end, and if it's not cut off, it will actually crawl up the hair strand. More and more of the hair gets weakened and damaged, until it eventually breaks off. This creates the illusion that your hair isn't growing because any progress you're making from the top is being broken off by the bottom.

Make trims part of your beauty lifestyle. Get them every 8-12 weeks.

Now, I know trims have been a traumatizing experience for some of us. A conversation I would encourage you to have with your stylist would be discussing the long and short term goals for your hair, agreeing on a plan you both can commit to, and agreeing on how much hair to trim at each appointment. Is it all the damage, or is it a specific measurement of length coming off? Then have your stylist show you what they see, because a technical inch to us may feel like 5 to you, and the damage we are trained to see may not be a comfortable length for you. Trims are good. Don't be scared.

Use a leave-in moisturizer before brushing

Leave-in moisturizers, sometimes called leave-in conditioners, are used to help detangle the hair and lock in the moisture. Use it on the ends and middle of damp or dry hair before brushing it out and styling.

This makes for easier brushing and will protect your hair against damage from styling. It is recommended to use this product any time you are brushing your hair. These products are lightweight and should not weigh down the hair if used multiple times throughout the week.

If you have fine hair (or need something for your kids) use a spray. If you have coarse, thick, or curly hair, you'll want to use a leave-in that has more of a lotion-like consistency.

Do not use it as a replacement for in-shower daily conditioner.

Leave-in's act as little barrier protectors that help aid in brushing while locking in moisture you gained from conditioning in the shower.

It is not the same as a conditioner used after shampoo.

Master the art of blow drying

Blow drying helps prepare the hair for a style. When you blow-dry your hair, you seal the hair's cuticle. Smoothing out the hair, locks in those keratin bonds and sets the hair in the position that you want it in, prolonging and protecting the style.

Start by using a heat protectant.
We put our hair through a lot—brushing, drying, sun damage, free radicals in the air, not to mention our constant playing with and styling. Any added protection does wonders! We want our hair to gain the styling benefits from using heat without inflicting any of the damage, which a thermal protectant* brilliantly does. Apply and brush through damp hair before blow drying or just before heat styling.

For smoothing out hair:

Use this technique when you want a straighter, smoother look to the hair. It also really helps seal the cuticle and lock in moisture.

It can be done on any hair type. The thicker and coarser the hair, the more time it will take.

- Towel dry your hair, so it's not dripping wet.
- Apply a leave-in conditioner to detangle and retain moisture, a thermal protectant to block the hair from heat damage, and a blow dry cream* to aid in styling.
- Then brush through the hair.

As a general note, blow dry creams are only needed if you are trying to smooth out your hair with a blow dryer. They are applied before you begin drying, so that it dries with your hair. They are heat activated and designed to help you smooth out the hair and hold the style you are about to create. You don't need a lot. Only use enough to evenly distribute throughout the hair.

A good way to tell if you are using too much of this product is to take a section of hair and run a comb through it after you apply the product. Then look at the comb to see if there is a white residue on the bristles. If there is, that means the comb is picking up too much product. You can add a section of hair that does not have any product in it to this section and comb the two together to distribute the extra product.

When blow drying to smooth out the hair, I recommend getting a *concentrator for your blow dryer. This is an attachment that goes on the end of your blow dryer. The concentrator nozzle directs and intensifies the strength of the air flow, which gives you more control and can cut down drying time, making the process of smoothing out your hair a great deal easier.

Using the blow dryer and your hands, you're going to rough dry the hair until it's only slightly damp. In the rough dry stage, your hair should be moving, so pick up sections of your hair that are light enough for the blow dryer to move on its own. It's okay if your hair looks like it is in a tornado. You want to throw your hair around. Use your hands to brush through sections of your hair and flip it back and forth.

When your hair is slightly damp, introduce the round brush. These brushes are cylinder shaped with bristles all the way around them, and are used to create tension in order to smooth out the hair. The size of the brush is based on the length of the hair. If you can wrap a section of hair all the way around the brush, it will be good to use. The shorter the hair, the smaller the brush. The bristles are there to create tension on the hair. These are what will pull the hair taunt and help straighten out the hair as it dries. The thicker or coarser the hair, the more bristles you need.

When picking out a round brush, you don't want it to glide through the hair super easily. You want it to just have a slight tug that will get you the tension you need.

Separate the hair into easy use partings—for example back to front, or bottom to top. Grab a section that is about 1-2 inches thick. You should be able to feel airflow from the blow dryer all the way through that section of hair.

You can also measure that section with the bristles of your round brush. The bristles should reach all the way through the hair. If you can't see the bristles, the section is too thick. For width, keep the hair in line with the bristle part of the brush. If the hair reaches past where the bristles end (like toward the handle), that section is too wide.

Clip away the other sections to keep things organized. Concentrating on one section at a time, put the round brush under the section of hair with the blow dryer above, sandwiching the hair in the middle.

Use the brush to create tension in the hair. Move the blow dryer and brush down the hair together in the same motion. This will close the hair's cuticle and give the hair a shiny, smooth finish.

Repeat this same motion on that section of hair until the hair is fully dry. If you can get your round brush all the way through the section without any tugging or stop-up's, that's usually a good indicator that the section is done.

Don't use an excessive amount of product or have your heat on so high your hair begins to smoke. A little steam from heat here and there is okay, but a continuous emitting of smoke is usually a sign that too much product is left in the hair or that the blow dryer is too hot.

Getting good at blow drying will take practice, so be patient with yourself. The more practice you put in, the quicker you will be at it.

For drying curly hair:

Use this technique when you want to keep the curl pattern that you have, seal the cuticle, and lock in moisture.

First off, leave the hair with some moisture in it. Don't rush to towel dry it.

Also, you may find it beneficial to not actually use a towel, but an old t-shirt, or something that is typically 100% cotton, soft, and smooth. Using a towel on curly hair can almost be like using velcro to dry it.

Apply a leave-in conditioner to detangle and retain moisture, a thermal protectant to block the hair from heat damage, and a curl product to aid in styling and then brush through the hair while the hair is still damp, or even wet.

Your hair's curl pattern (wavey, cury, tight coil etc.) will determine the type of curl product you get. The label on the product should tell you what type of curl it is for. Grab the one that matches your curl type. You want products that lock in the moisture, fight frizz, and hold your curl.

Blow drying for curly hair is called *diffusing.

Using a diffuser attachment on your blow dryer is key. This attachment goes on the end of the blowdryer and looks like a circular plate with smooth, little spikes poking out of it. It disperses the airflow from the blow dryer and helps accentuate your curl pattern.

Grabbing a section of hair, place the ends of the hair onto the diffuser and push or scrunch the curls toward the scalp.

The section should be thin enough to feel the air flow all the way through it and small enough to fit on the diffuser.

Leave it there for about 15 seconds then adjust and do the same motion throughout the head until the hair is dry.

You do not need super high airflow and should have your blow dryer set on medium to high heat.

Go over sections more than once, separating the hair with your fingers, and flipping them back and forth to diffuse at different angles. This can help with volume and mixing of sections, so the hair overall blends together.

Flipping your head upside down can also help with added volume on top.

Some people like to pull on the sections slightly towards the end when the hair is almost completely dry to separate the curls a little more.

Getting good at diffusing will take practice, so be patient with yourself. The more practice you put in, the quicker you will be at it.

Air Drying

Air-drying is a preferred technique if you want less styling time and to keep the hair's natural wave or curl pattern.

Leave the hair with some moisture in it, and towel dry it just enough so that it is not dripping wet.

Apply a leave-in conditioner to detangle and retain moisture and an oil to really protect the ends. Brush these through the hair.

A styling product can be added to help with frizz prevention. If your hair has some type of wave or curl pattern to it, I recommend getting a styling product for your specific wave pattern. This will help in holding the style after the hair is dry.

After you have distributed these products through the hair, you can leave it as is if your hair is on the straighter side, or scrunch it to get the desired curl before allowing it to dry.

If your hair is damaged or really delicate, I recommend blow drying it. When hair is wet it's also the most fragile because the strands swell and the protein in the hair forms a less strong hydrogen bond. When it's dry however, those bonds become keratin bonds, forming a stronger seal and protection for the hair.

Curly hair

Another recommendation for curly hair is sleeping with a silk pillow, silk cap or scarf. This is a protective measure for how delicate curly hair can be. Sleeping with a silk pillow, cap, or scarf will keep your hair from getting thrashed around at night and becoming more damaged or tangled. Doing this will also protect your hair's natural oils.

Heat styling

Heat styling should be done on dry hair only and with a thermal protectant.

You can blow dry this in or mist lightly on hair that is already dry, and wait a minute or two for it to completely dry before using a hot tool. Any leftover moisture still in your hair will intensify heat damage and potentially even fry your hair.

If your hair is falling flat too quickly after a curl, or not staying straight after using a flat iron, it typically means that not enough product is being used to hold that style.

Styling products can be added to help define the shape and hold the style you are about to create. I recommend you blow dry these into your hair.

After styling, if the hair is not exposed to moisture, or being tampered with, it should last you at least until the next day, potentially even until you wash it.

I recommend getting a heat tool that tells you the actual temperature (avoid the tools with those "low, medium, high" settings). This will give you more control and help prevent the heat from becoming too hot.

As a general rule of thumb, you should be between 200-360 degrees Fahrenheit. The coarser the hair, the higher the temperature needed. I know most curling irons and flat irons go up to 450 degrees, but that's typically used to activate a treatment, and should only be done in the salon.

You should be holding an iron on your hair for eight to fifteen seconds max.

Take smaller sections when curling. When straightening, make sure the iron is continuously moving. It is better to use less heat and more passes, than less passes with more heat.

When the hair is smooth and has a slight sheen to it, the cuticle has sealed and the iron does not need to be left on any longer.

Using too high of heat, leaving the iron on the hair too long, or heat styling too often can burn the hair and ruin it's natural curl pattern.

When using any heat tool, make sure that all the hair in that section is actually touching the iron. If not all the hair is making contact with the iron, that section is too thick.

When using a curling iron, note that the bigger the barrel the looser the curl.

When holding the iron horizontally, it will give you a wider bouncier curl.

When holding the iron vertically the curl will be elongated, thinner, and closer to a wave.

Pro tip: For more control, I recommend over-curling the hair, then brushing it out to the desired level of curl or wave. This will make the style last longer.

Use hairspray at the end of a hairstyle.

Use hairspray at the end of styling to lock in and finish your look.

Spray it at an arm's length away, and layer it on for added strength. Hair spray is meant to mist on the hair, whether in liquid form or aerosol, forming a light, dry layer of hold. If applied too close, or too much at one time, the hair spray can dampen the hair too much and compromise the style.

Don't use before heat styling. Hairsprays are a finishing product, designed to lock in and capture the longevity of a style. You want hairspray to be the last thing you use, not the first.

Hairsprays come in liquid or aerosol, and range from light hold to freezing a style in place.

For a down style with more movement, or to help with little fly aways, a light hairspray can be used.

For updos with the need for a longer lasting style, you can opt for a stronger hold.

How to use dry shampoo

Dry shampoos should be applied at the root of your hair. They remove excess oil from the scalp, add volume to your hair, and get you an extra day (maybe 2) out of styling. Dry shampoos absorb any moisture or oils that cause weight to the root area, which typically adds much more volume to a style. They're perfect for a last minute pick me up before you go out.

Do not use it as a replacement for a normal shampoo washing routine.

Dry shampoos are a quick style fix, not a quick clean fix.

Although they can make limp hair look amazing, they also can cause added build up and should not be left on longer than a couple days. It is made to hold you over until you can wash your hair, not replace a wash.

Our hair is our glory, whatever style you decide to wear and display. My hope is that these tips will help you take care of your hair and set it up in the most healthy and beautiful way. In this next chapter, we will get down in the details of all things makeup, and best practices to make it healthy and incredibly fun.

Questions from Your Beauty Godmother

1. *What is a goal you have for your hair?*

It could be to grow longer, get rid of damage, or maybe even try a new style.

2. *What is something from this chapter you can implement to bring more life and health to your hair?*

It can be maybe investing in a professional grade product, trying a new styling technique, or designing a plan with your hairstylist.

Chapter 8
The Magic of Makeup

What role does makeup play?

Makeup is not always necessary. Makeup is part of hygiene. Are you taking care of yourself? Are you doing your eyebrows?

Makeup is a tool. When you're getting really dressed up, you will feel more comfortable at a gala if you're wearing makeup. You feel more comfortable in an on camera interview if you're wearing makeup. It's not the same type of makeup, but it's a tool for the arena you're in to set you up for success.

You don't need to wear it every day, especially if that's not who you are. If you're a tomboy, wearing makeup in your everyday life might not be an extension of your true identity, but when you're in professional settings, you can use it as a tool to create a softer appearance that can elevate you in a particular social circle.

Makeup has endless possibilities, and it's incredibly fun! It should be something you know how to use for when you want to. You shouldn't be flustered or intimidated by it. For those occasions when you do want to wear makeup, this is how you can use it as a tool to feel more confident and set yourself up for success.

Wash your face

"Makeup only looks as good as the skin underneath."
-Stole that from a M.A.C educator.

Although I do advise talking with your esthetician about what kind of regimen you should have for your skin type, cleansing your face in the morning and evening essentially creates a "blank canvas" to work with when applying makeup. It allows skin to breathe, rejuvenate, and prevents breakouts. Yes, blemishes can be covered up, and there are amazing products to help with that, but don't make yourself work harder than you need too.

Don't leave makeup on overnight.

Leaving makeup on overnight keeps the skin from breathing which can cause clogged pores and breakouts. It also prematurely ages the skin. This is practically a makeup sin in the makeup artist world. In beauty school, they told us every night with makeup left on the skin ages it anywhere from 3-7 days. In an even scarier experiment conducted in 2013 by the Daily Mail, a woman stopped washing her face for an entire month. She reapplied her makeup over her unwashed skin each morning. The results: experts said she literally aged herself by 10 years![1]

Brushes

There is an endless array of makeup brushes, but I will walk you through the basics.

- A dense brush: Big or small, is great for applying makeup like foundation, or eyeshadow. This type of brush is typically used in slower, broad sweeping motions.

- A fluffy brush: Big or small, is great for *blending, transitioning one color to another, or removing harsh lines, these are typically used in light sweeping or circular motions.

- A sharper brush: Used for creating defined or sharper lines, think about liners, or cat eyes. These are designed for you to be able to use as you would a pen or small paint brush.

Generally speaking, the size of the brush can also help you determine what the brush is for. Big brushes, for example, that can cover the width of your cheek or forehead are used for face makeup because they cover more surface area.

A brush that can fit within the hollows of your cheeks is generally used for *contouring, blush, or highlight.

---

[1] (https://www.dailymail.co.uk/femail/article-2380419/What-sleeping-make-does-skin-Our-shocking-experiment-exposes-happens.html)

A small brush that can fit within the lid of your eye is typically used for the eye area.

Match your foundation to your body

Think of the overall picture. Just as you would want the tan on your arms to match your legs, you also want your face to match your body. The best practice when looking for a foundation is to match it to your chest/collarbone area. Be sure to blend whatever foundation you apply down to your neck to avoid a harsh line. Blend to your neck; don't match to your neck. Blend the foundation from your face down into your neck, so that you have a smooth transition from your face to your neck, no hash lines or cut offs.

Don't match your foundation color to your neck.

Your neck always has a shadow cast over it. Because it's positioned under and farther from the highpoints of your face, it will never match your face exactly—which is totally fine! We just want a smooth transition between the two. Even in big fancy photoshoots, the makeup artists don't try to match the neck exactly because the model would look flat and weird—like she has no neck. This is why you want to match your foundation to your chest (or if you want to sound really fancy, the *décolleté).

Do not apply foundation with your bare hands.

You can blend out a small last minute area or delicate area with your finger. However, applying foundation with your fingers can be more harmful than helpful.

First, the skin on your hand will absorb just as much makeup as your face, and we don't want to waste precious makeup. Second, the oils, not to mention any germs left on your hand, will be added to your makeup and skin on your face, which could actually cause the makeup to oxidize* faster or change consistency. Third, it just makes a big mess.

Use an applicator suitable to your skin type. There are many different types of applicators to choose from, which can feel overwhelming, but we're going to say it's exciting. You get to find the perfect tool that's just for you! Declare goodness.

Applicators, such as brushes, beauty blenders, or silicones, not only help apply foundation, but also help blend, *buff, and smooth out the skin's look.

- Brushes are an original favorite, and the easiest to use. You hold them the way you would a pen or paint brush, so they have a sense of familiarity. They are especially good for textured skin, as they blend and set the makeup into the skin while applying.

- Beauty blenders are meant to blend (although some people use it to apply as well) because they are soft, and the micro sponge texture mimics that of your skin. If you use a beauty blender, make sure to dampen the sponge with water or a setting spray before applying any makeup product. The water will keep the sponge from absorbing too much foundation, which leaves more for your skin.

- Silicones are great applicators. They absorb zero product, so you save a ton in the long run. Typically, you can cut in half the amount you would use with a brush application. The technique takes some getting used to however. Because it is silicone, it can pull on the skin if there is not enough product or moisture. A silicone requires more of a spreading and smoothing motion, rather than brushing or patting.

All are great mediums, and I, as a makeup artist, use all three. I encourage you to find what is most comfortable for you.

Use your brows to frame your face

Your eyebrows are not meant to dominate your face.

A simple way to create and measure out the shape of your eyebrows at home is to take a straight device, like a pen, ruler, or eyeliner pencil, and using your nose as the base, put the bottom of your pen at your nose.

- First, starting on one side, line your ruler or pen up with the outside of your nostril, going vertically straight up toward your hairline. The point at that line and where your eyebrows cross is generally where your eyebrows should start.

- Leaving the base of the pen at the outside of your nostril, slant the pen to make a diagonal line from your nose through the center of your eyeball out to your hairline. The point at which that line and your eyebrows cross here is generally where your arch should be. This should be the highest point of your eyebrow and your starting point.

- Leaving the base of the pen where it is, slant it further, so the bottom touches the base of your nose and passes the outer corner of your eye out to your hairline. The point where this line and your eyebrows cross is where your eyebrow should generally end. This should be the lowest point of your eyebrow.

- Connect the starting point to the arch, and the arch to the end. This should give you a framework to the shape of your brow.

- Fill in the bottom of your brow, then lightly blend up towards the top for a full, yet natural, look. You can add arch sharpness and overall fullness to your brow as you feel comfortable.

Don't drag or use heavy long strokes. When drawing on or filling in your eyebrows, use small, light strokes for a softer, natural look. Think of mimicking all the little hairs that make up your eyebrow.

Unless you are going for a total comic look, heavier solid colors can make the brow look very painted on and unnatural. The heavier the look, the more attention it draws away from your eye. We want the brows to accentuate your face's natural beauty and show off your fabulous eyes.

Do not try to match eyebrow color exactly to hair color

Blondes: use 1-2 shades darker than hair color.
Brunettes: use 1-2 shades lighter than hair color.

Typically blondes can barely see the hair on their brow or lash-line. Going a shade or two darker will help define the brow area without looking unnatural.

The hair on brunettes, however, usually stands out. Using a color 1-2 shades lighter, you can define shape or fill in any sparse areas without making the brow darker or harsher. A shade lighter also makes the brow area feel softer and lighter– angelic, if you will.

Don't try to match your eyebrow color exactly to your hair color.

Oftentimes, this ends up being too harsh or dark on the face. The brow's hairs are less dense and not as thick as the hair on your head anyway. No matter your desired shape for your brow, the goal is something soft and natural.

Use *matte pigments when mastering the contour

Contour brings shape to the face by creating intentionally placed shadows. Matte pigments are essential because they don't *shimmer. *Real life shadows don't shimmer.*

Look for contour palettes, or a shade of contour, about two shades darker than your foundation.

Look for sunken points in the cheek area, typically right under the cheek bone, or in the temples and just under the chin bone (not the eye sockets). Apply with a medium sized fluffy brush (if it's a powder) or a dense brush (for a cream) in soft sweeping motions. The size of your brush should measure about the same as the hollow of your cheek (the space between your cheekbone and jawline). Contour should blend out towards the cheekbone and jaw. There should not be a sharp line.

Don't use shimmery or *warm toned pigments.

A shimmer (or warm tone) counteracts the goal of a contour. A contour should bring shape and depth to the face and almost fall in the background to let other things shine, like the highpoints of the cheekbone or your eye. Leave the warmth to blush and shimmer to *highlight.

The role of bronzer

Bronzer is used to make the skin look glowy and more tan. You see this being used a lot during the summer. This is typically brushed across long surfaces, cheekbones, jawline, sometimes the forehead or even neck & collar bone area. When applying you can use a large fluffy brush, similar to the size of your foundation brush.

Bronzer is typically a shade or two darker than natural skin tone, which is sometimes why people confuse the two when shopping. Bronzer usually has a shimmer, is on the warmer side, and typically is sold as a stand alone product, while contour products are usually sold in kits with two shades, or are paired with a highlight shade.

Only use highlighter on highpoints

Treat highlighter as sacred. Use the glorious gift of the highlighter on the cheekbones, nose bridge, under eyebrow arches, and cupid's bow *only*.

Opposite to the contour, for a highlight we want these parts of your face to stand out. Let the light shine on these areas. Lightly dust across the highpoints of the face. This should also be subtle.

Don't blend into or spread over your whole face.

We want shadows (low points) and focal points (highpoints) specifically placed. This creates shape and accentuates the face's natural features. Spreading a highlight across larger areas defeats that effect and can also make the face look flat, or worse, like a disco ball.

When choosing a highlight color, warmer tones typically look softer and more natural. However, some women do not like the warm tone, or feel like their face looks red.

I recommend a more pearly tone for fair skin. This will usually have a soft white look, sometimes with hints of a light pink.

If you have more medium to deeper toned skin, I recommend highlights with a gold element, and deeper copper warmth.

Apply blush subtlety

Blush, sometimes called rouge, should be subtle, even when using a bold color. Apply it just to the cheekbones (the apple of your cheek) and softly blend out to create warmth and bring femininity to the face. It can *maybe be* applied to the eyelid, or onto moisturized lips if you really love the color—but even then, subtlety is key.

Don't run the blush across the rest of the face.

Blush can very easily be overdone. It is not meant to be the focal point. It is meant to help the face not look so washed out, and give a girly, flirty edge to your overall look. It's the backup singer to your Beyoncé. You want to hear words like "glowing," "dewy," "fresh faced," and "youthful looking." If you hear compliments like that, you know blush has done its job without stealing the show.

When picking a color, pick tones that match the depth of your skin. For example, if you have fairer skin, you should use lighter pinks, something you would see at a baby shower or on a ballet slipper. Medium skin tones will lean more towards peachy, coral, or deeper pinks like bubblegum. Deeper skin tones will use deeper pigments like ruby reds, fuchsia, and magenta, sometimes even orange.

Eyeshadow

Eyeshadow has endless options. With any eye color, you can never go wrong with a natural colored palette, but here are some general guides when looking for eyeshadows based on your eye color.

- **Blue eye color**: Blue is a cool tone, so warmer colors will contrast it best. There are also purple, taupe/earth tones (like deep brown), slate grays, light pinks (like rose), and metallics that look really good with blue eyes.

- **Brown eye color**: Deeper colors typically accentuate brown eyes really well. Other colors like gold, peach, coral, plum purples, greens, and grays can also look really nice.

- **Green eye color**: Purples and taupes can really make green eyes pop because they are opposite on the color spectrum, golds, coppers, warm oranges, and warm browns can also be really pretty.

- **Hazel eye color**: Hazel is in the middle between green and brown eyes, which means you can pull from both those shades.

Keep in mind that a lot of these colors will be affected by your skin tone and overall preference. You are also not limited to these colors based on your eye color. They are just a good place to start. A lot of companies sell palettes with different look books attached, that almost give you a color by number step guide on which colors to use and where to place them on the eye. You can get really creative. I would recommend playing with different looks and seeing what you feel most comfortable and confident in.

If you are playing with more than one color, I recommend starting with the lightest color you plan on using first, then add in the darker colors one step at a time. A dense brush will be optimal for applying the color. If you are trying to soften the line or end of where you applied the color, a fluffier brush will help you do this. Use the fluffy brush in light circular motions.

Become a lash queen

Curling is meant to bring shape, while the mascara is meant to lock it in and add volume. Curl before applying mascara. I know it can be intimidating. The curler is only meant for the top lashes. Relax, be gentle, and take your time practicing. Position your lashes in between the clamps of the curler. Get as close to the lash line as possible without getting your eyelid. Some women use the top of the curler to push away the skin and rest the curler on the eyelid to get to the base of the lashes. *Gently* clasp down until the lashes fold up. You should feel a little tug on your lashes, but not enough to hurt. Clamp down, then release your lashes completely *before* pulling away from your eye. Pull the curler away from your eye and examine the shape of your lashes. You can do this process a few times until you have the desired shape.

Here are some tips to help apply mascara like a pro:

- Curl your lashes with an eyelash curler all the way up, not just at the base. This creates a corner with a very angular shape. Curl beginning at the base, then another curl in the middle and another at the ends for a full shape (think of the letter "C" or an ocean wave).

- Use a waterproof mascara if you find your curl isn't holding, if there is a lot of humidity, or if you're expecting to cry (this is key at weddings).

- Try wiggling the mascara wand slightly side to side at the base of the lash, then sweep through to the ends to help with coverage and separation.

- This step may be my favorite, try using an old credit card! Place it in between your lashes and eyelid to avoid getting mascara on that masterpiece of eyeshadow you just created.

Different mascara brushes are designed for the different types of lashes, based on what you have and the result you want. Some offer more length, while others build volume.

The label will tell you which are meant to do what. You can also always use two separate mascaras as well.

Don't wait for mascara to completely dry before applying another layer.

If you're trying to build volume or length in your lash, and are using more than one coat, don't wait for the coats to completely dry before reapplying. Maybe give it 30 seconds to start to dry and form, but don't wait much longer than that. When too much "dry" mascara is applied, it can cause a lot of clumping (the spider leg lash), ball on the ends of the lash, and/or flake and fall out on the rest of your face. Applying the coats of mascara closer together will keep everything smooth and feathery, which is what you want for your flirty lashes.

Questions from Your Beauty Godmother

1. *What is a goal you have for the area of makeup?*

It could be mastering a new technique, to become confident in curling your lashes, or seeing a esthetician and getting a healthy skin regime.

2. *What is something from this chapter you can implement to bring more fun or skill to your makeup routine?*

It can be playing with new colors, or trying new looks throughout the week.

Chapter 9
The Magic in You

By now I'm sure you know this book is not a "fix it all before the clock strikes twelve" Cinderella fairytale prescription. The beauty you discovered is a lifestyle. It's a deep rooted identity you get to develop and grow with through every season. You had to fight through a lot to get here. Some of these truths might have been hard to hear, but you chose to lay down your insecurities and fight through negative mindsets. You chose to follow the crazy Beauty Godmother and open the door to new beliefs—to get really real about the person you see and the person you are meant to be. Now it's time to begin the work of bringing that vision into your day to day reality.

I hope you know your beauty, love yourself, and are excited about what you bring to the world. It pains me to see women speak negatively about themselves, not truly understanding what they have to offer and how amazing they are. It breaks my heart every time I hear about a woman feeling insecure, looking in the mirror and only being able to see things they don't like. Oppositely, I cannot explain the joy I feel when I see women (when I see you) walking in confidence—not the pretend pretty persona you muster up and stage to the world, but the real beautiful you. The one who loves how you are designed. The one who loves living the way you are made to be.

I pray you can be that beauty, the one who is powerful and soft, gracious and gentle. I pray that you are firm in your identity, in tune with the world around you, and confident in what you bring to every situation. I pray you will be a woman who is guiding others into wisdom, freedom, and the best versions of themselves—the type of woman who gets more beautiful with time and purer layer by layer.

Beauty that is thrilling to the sight and healing to the heart—this is true beauty.

It goes beyond trends or age. This beauty is something to be admired. Because of this, it's also a target for attack, but it is so fierce. Unbothered by ever changing opinions, it doesn't compare itself to other people and doesn't depend on validation from others. Instead, true beauty affirms other people. This resilience makes this beauty untouchable. This way of life, way of being, it's in every sunrise, wildflower, and raging storm. It's in you. It is you.

You are this beauty. You are this woman. I believe it.

The magic is that now, you believe it too.

Love,

Your Beauty Godmother

Glossary

Astringent: A harsh cleaning and constricting substance, diminishes oil, or moisture based liquids. Is typically medicinal and/or used for a specific purpose.

Blend: To mix, inseparably together. When blending as in color or makeup, there should be a smooth transition from where one color ends to when another begins, no harsh lines.

Blow dry cream: A product applied before blow drying hair, that aid's in the smoothing of the hair, as well as providing extra hold and longevity to the style.

Buff: To clean or polish/ shine. When buffing in makeup, you are polishing and removing texture, or any grainlike finish.

Concentrator: A blow dryer attachment that sits on the end of a blow dryer nozzle, helps to concentrate and direct the airflow.

Contour: To outline or bring shape to.

Cool tone: Shades of green, blue, and purple. Any shade with an undertone of green, blue, or purple is a cool color. Opposite of warm tones.

Décolleté (day·kowl·tey): A french word, describing the area including neck and shoulders.

Diffusing: A term used in haircare to describe the process of drying curly hair with a blowdryer. Typically will use a diffuser attachment on the blow dryer that disperses the air flow.

Fashion Tone: Is a term used in hair care to describe an unnaturally produced color, fire truck reds, metallics, or pastel toned colors are not natural hair colors.

Glitter: A bold sparkle particle. Glitter stands alone and is sold as an individual product. It's very bold, and almost impossible to mute or blend out. The actual product is bigger than a shimmer as well. Shimmer is subtle and blends into the product. Glitter can be mixed in, but your eye will see the actual glitter particle.

Highlight: To emphasize or make prominent, make brighter.

Matte: A color or tone with no shine elements.

Over-Proteinized: When hair has an overload of protein, it can cause the hair to look and feel more brittle.

Oxidize: As it refers to makeup, is the drying of, or color changing of foundation. Very similar to when an avocado turns brown after being cut open. It is a chemical process, ingredients in the foundation reacting to oxygen, or natural oils in the skin.

Shimmer: Having a sparkly element. A small particle that adds a shine or sparkle, incorporated into the color. Think of sand. When you pick up a handful, you can see all the different pigmentations and variations. It sparkles in the sunlight, but you can't separate or pick apart each pigment, or take the shiny parts out. When a product or color is shimmery there is a general sparkle that is more subtle than glitter.

Shine: Anything that reflects light. Typically the difference between lip gloss and lipstick. Lip gloss has a shine to it, and almost looks wet. Lipstick does not have a shine to it, and looks more dry. Shimmer and glitter have a shiny component to them.

Smooth: To remove projections, ridges, or wrinkles. Getting rid of unevenness or roughness.

Thermal protectant: A product used in hair care to protect the hair from any damage produced by heat exposure.

Warm tone: Shades of yellow, red, and orange. Any shade of yellow, red or orange is a warm tone. Opposite of cool tones.

Thank you for Reading
Love, Your Beauty Godmother

Reviews help books get discovered, so if you enjoyed the content, please let us know your thoughts on all the bookseller websites!

Did you try a makeup look or hairstyle and feel absolutely fabulous?

Tag us in your next selfie or video!
IG: @the.beautygodmother

www.loveyourbeautygodmother.com

Acknowledgements

To the tribe of women who believed in me, encouraged me to write, and walked me through this process. You all collectively had a hand in building *The Beauty Godmother* and giving her a voice.

I would like to thank Fiona for being the person who called out a book from within me. Alyssa for coaching me through this process and making it a tangible reality. Tony and Alisa for encouraging me along the way, and always being available to be guideposts and share their own journey being authors. Thank you to Carissa and Bella for being my creative minds and building a brand with me. Thank you to all the people who were a part of the beta reading and editing process. Your feedback and communication created a language of beauty throughout this book.

About the Author

Blyss Macias has been a hair stylist and makeup artist for 10+ years, operating her own business, The Industry, for nearly half that time. In addition to helping people feel like the most fabulous versions of themselves, she's also worked with everyone from beauty pageants, to professional fitness competitors, to international speakers. Blyss is extremely passionate about helping women embody the beauty they inherently have within themselves and is on a mission to change the way the world sees beauty– from an image to an essence and lifestyle.

In addition to helping people live as the truest version of themselves, Blyss is also a lowkey fitness junkie and foodie who loves to hangout at the beach and create epic playlists.

Made in the USA
Las Vegas, NV
25 November 2022

60241924R00072